At the
ARROYO'S
EDGE

Flowing waters worked their way freely down the Arroyo before construction of the present drainage system.

At the ARROYO'S EDGE

A
HISTORY
OF
LINDA
VISTA

By Beverly Wayte

*Historical Society of
Southern California
and Linda Vista/Annandale
Association
Los Angeles, 1993*

This work was originally published in serial form in *Southern California Quarterly*, vol. LXXIII, 2-4, with the title "Linda Vista Revisited: From Indian Days to Modern Pasadenans."

Contents

Foreword, by Barry H. Herlihy 1
Introduction 5
1. Indians, Spaniards and Rancho San Rafael . . . 9
2. A Prelude and a Boom 21
3. After the Boom 37
4. Life Goes On 45
5. Transition 55
6. Sustaining the Garden Paradise 67
7. An Assemblage of Noted Residents. 81
8. Architecture and Homes 93
Acknowledgments. 96
Notes 97
Index 101
Acknowledgments 112

Illustrations

Flowing waters in the Arroyo . . . . . . *frontispiece*
Map showing Indian camps in the Arroyo, 1860 8
One of the Verdugo adobes, 1857 12
Deseño of Rancho La Cañada 15
Joseph Lancaster Brent 16
Alfred Beck Chapman and O.W. Childs 18
Moses Langley Wicks 20
A lush and woodsy Arroyo 25
Looking west across the Arroyo, 1900 28
Looking towards Linda Vista across the Arroyo 32
Looking towards upper Linda Vista 35
Pasadena's Monk Hill 39
Linda Vista, looking north to Yokum's ranch 40
Mr. Blake and his bee hives 44
Dorn family farm house 46
Looking west across the Arroyo to Annandale 47
Looking west across Brookside Park 47
Views of Linda Vista, 1905 48
The Hoffman homestead and El Mirador Dairy 51
A view of the present site of the Rose Bowl, 1905 54
Clarence Day 57
Looking west across the Arroyo, 1910 58
Scoville bridge, dam and pump house 59
Site of the future B.O. Kendall estate 61
The Pegfair estate 65
Demolition of the Linda Vista bridge 72
Art Center College of Design 76
The El Mirador Ranch development, 1987 79
Elmer Wachtel 83
James Scripps Booth residence 85
Dr. Frederick Webb Hodge 89
Wachtel painting, "Spend Your Life on the Verandah" 94

Foreword

I am pleased to have this opportunity to introduce to you another excellent example of southern California local history. I believe you will find Beverly Wayte's *At the Arroyo's Edge* informative and enriching whether you live in Linda Vista, as I do, or elsewhere.

To understand what is happening to our southern California community at large, one must look not only at the often discouraging urban landscape around us, but also at the history of our region. Perhaps then we can better appreciate how important it is to maintain the livability of a place, and how much is lost when not enough is done to ensure that livability.

Many of us are not from "here," we simply pass through, often taking more from the community than we add to it, and then move on. We give little thought to the neighborhoods where we live and work, and even less to their history. Not surprisingly, we fail to develop the sense of place and being that such knowledge imparts. That might have been my fate were it not for my father.

I am a native Angeleno, but my father grew up on a ranch in New Mexico with three of his brothers. They were part of the westward migration, having left the city life of New York in 1908 for the wilds of the Llano Estacado. In their case, it was a migration which began with the departure of their mother from Germany in the 1860s and of their late father's parents from Ireland during the Famine.

Although my father left school half way through the sixth grade, he was fortunate. While there was no school close enough to attend in New Mexico, his mother and brothers were avid readers and brought with them more books than other baggage. He continued his education reading those books and eventually graduated from the University of Arizona first in his law school class. His was a lifelong love of learning, which included an intense interest in history.

He imparted that love of history to me. He had a great ability to recall both what he had read and experienced, thus preserving much of our family history and tying it to the local history of places where the family had lived. I was part of his audience and eventually, when he recorded it, one of his readers. To this day many of the people and places he described remain very real to me.

When I moved to Linda Vista in 1975, to a house on Chamberlain Road, I discovered my own connection with its history. My father asked if I remembered the house my uncle had built more than fifty years earlier on Linda Vista Avenue, just a few blocks away. I then realized it was perhaps that subconscious connection with Linda Vista which drew me back many years later.

Before I read Beverly Wayte's history when it first appeared in the *Southern California Quarterly,* I had only limited knowledge of what it was that made Linda Vista so special. Although she focuses on a mere hillside, one descending from the Verdugo mountains on the west to the Arroyo Seco on the east, it is a focus that held my attention. I thought of all the diverse energies that went into the making of this small bedroom community outside of Los Angeles and I came away pleased with the new sense of place and of belonging which I received from her history.

At the Arroyo's Edge incorporates all of the movements and passions of Southern California's past: native peoples, Alta California's Spanish involvement, mission and rancho influences, United States conquest, bountiful orchards, real estate boom and bust, Midwestern and Eastern entrepreneurs, and the joining of the arts with the environment. Linda Vista's history has it all!

Histories such as this convey more than dry facts to the reader. As someone once said: "The facts of local history are meant to become an integral part of our own life. They bring us closer to the past and, in so doing, bring us closer to the present; for we are living history as well as recording it, and our memories are as necessary as our anticipations."

To Beverly Wayte, and to all those who have made this publication possible, history enthusiasts in general and the people of Linda Vista in particular owe their gratitude. *At the Arroyo's Edge* makes a valuable contribution to the rich tapestry of local history in southern California.

Barry H. Herlihy
Executive Director
The Village Museum at Heritage Square

Introduction

Linda Vista lies three miles northwest of Pasadena, upon the west bank of the Arroyo Seco—a collection of houses shadowed by the San Rafael Hills that rise beyond. Here are the Park Place nursery and the Forestry Commission experimental station; but to the tourist the chief interest will perhaps centre in the trail that leads up over the hills just before we come to Linda Vista, by which the highest peak of the San Rafael range is reached, two thousand feet in height. The location of the trail is marked by a small house upon the ridge and reservoir. . . . On the summit a cairn is found, the "post-office" where people from all over the world have left their cards and names in poetry and prose.

Charles Holder,
*All about Pasadena
and Its Vicinity* (1889)

Linda Vista stretches from Devil's Gate on the north to the Annandale section of Pasadena on the south and from the west bank of the Arroyo Seco to the ridge of the San Rafael Hills, a natural boundary between Pasadena and Glendale. The Linda Vista slopes, like all land south of the Tehachapi Mountains, are semi-desert and dependent upon rain. Relief from the heat is provided by wind from the west carrying moist air inland from the ocean.

The Linda Vista area has known many lives. Its history begins over one thousand years ago when Indians roamed the San Gabriel Valley, hunting for food, enjoying the climate, and erecting shelters. In 1542 Spanish explorers arrived in California led by Spanish adventurer Juan Rodriguez Cabrillo. The expedition landed in San Diego and then sailed up the coast, making contact with the Indians at various stops, including San Pedro. In 1769 a land expedition of soldiers led by Gaspar de Portolá arrived in the area, accompanied by Junípero Serra and Franciscan missionaries. Bent on making a Spanish colony of the land, they established presidios, pueblos and missions, and one of these missions was near Linda Vista.

The Mission San Gabriel was founded in 1771, near what is now Whittier Narrows, and then moved to its present site in 1775. At this time, soldiers and missionaries alike traveled the Arroyo Seco, using it as a trail from the old Monterey Road to the San Gabriel Mountains and then up the La Cañada Valley to destinations north.

In 1784 a large area west of the Arroyo was given as a Spanish land grant to José María Verdugo, one of Portolá's soldiers, and the hills were turned into grazing lands for cattle. Rancho San Rafael, as the land was eventually named, remained in the family of the original Spanish grantee until 1871, when the courts partitioned the rancho and sold it to speculators investing in the fabulous growth potential of southern California.

Midwestern settlers bought the land from the speculators and turned it into orchards and farmland, planting the Linda Vista hillsides with citrus trees. But by the early twentieth century, the orchards of Linda Vista began to disappear, making way for the entrepreneur's efforts to create a wealthy residential area with Italianate overtones.

As the years progressed, Linda Vista blended its former lives with the newer ones, evolving into its present state of a sequestered bedroom community, a medley of architectural styles amidst a lush, natural setting.

Although early photographs show the banks above the Arroyo relatively barren except for orchards, pioneers soon contributed other non-native trees such as eucalyptus, pepper and elm. Today the slopes abound with a variety of trees, and native flora covers the hillsides and gullies: oak, toyon, sycamore, sumac, sage, buckwheat and poppy. Squirrels leap among pines and birds burst out of small, rugged ravines. Crayola-colored flowers cascade from garden walls onto walks and lawns.

The 1980 census figures for the Linda Vista-Annandale area

show a population of 3,128 living in 1,250 houses. According to the Pasadena Planning Commission, the 1987 population estimate for the entire area is 3,425. The approximate number of houses for the same year is 1,274. This section of Pasadena is "characterized by having both the highest indexed median family income and housing unit value of any city area, making it the wealthiest area in the city while containing approximately 4%-5% of the city's population, housing units and households."[1]

Driving down tree-shaded Linda Vista Avenue, looking from right to left at expensive and well-maintained homes, it is difficult to imagine that a hundred years ago only a handful of farmers lived here. At that time, the one-lane, dirt road was bordered by newly planted pepper trees from nearby Park Nursery, and most of the residents spent their days in the fields tending infant fruit orchards, cutting alfalfa or gathering honey from beehives.

In 1889 Pasadena's chief public relations voice, Charles Frederick Holder, stated:

> At Pasadena the Arroyo forms a complete jungle, a most attractive resort for the walker or equestrian. Tall sycamore trees rear their graceful forms, while over the limbs and branches are festoons of the wild grape, clematis, and other vines, so luxuriant that they form a complete bower in many places. Live oaks, the willow, alder, and a variety of trees grow here, with vines and flowering plants innumerable, so that in the winter season the Arroyo becomes a literal garden.[2]

Homeowners continue to live in Linda Vista for the very reasons Holder mentions: parents find the bucolic area ideal for raising children, commuters find tonic in the peaceful surroundings, and artists and scholars seek inspiration in the natural setting.

Linda Vista's history is elusive. Indians, cattlemen and farmers left scant documentation; furthermore, the land was not part of Pasadena until 1914, so early city records are of little help. Nonetheless, a reasonable record of events is obtainable from legal documents, local newspapers and some written accounts in order to tell a story of bold, risk-taking pioneers, wise investors and fantastic growth. The community emerges as a microscopic study of the 1880s boom era in southern California, and it offers a unique, personal history, well worth being recorded.

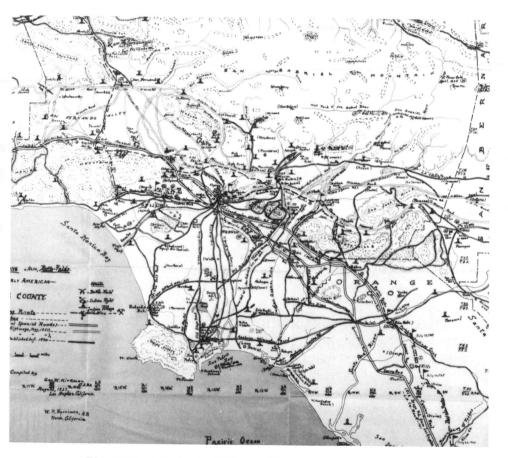

This 1938 rendering by Kirkman-Harriman shows Indian camps along the Arroyo about 1860. *(All photographs used to illustrate the text are courtesy Huntington Library unless otherwise noted.)*

CHAPTER ONE

Indians, Spaniards and Rancho San Rafael

"I'm a soldier of the king. All these hills are mine!
All these valleys and mesas are mine! All these
cattle are mine! I'm a soldier of the king!"
Words attributed to Julio
Verdugo by Hiram Reid in
History of Pasadena (1895).

When the Franciscan missionaries arrived with Spanish soldiers in Alta California, they named the various Indian groups
they found there according to the natives' proximity to newly
established missions. In this manner the Shoshonean family
of natives in whose neighborhood the Mission San Gabriel was
situated came to be called Gabrieliños.

Expedition diarists traveling with Portolá in 1769 wrote that
the Indians inhabiting the southern California valleys lived in
domed houses made from branches and grasses. Indian villages
were near springs and streams, which flourished more in those
days before concrete basins and dams proliferated in the area. One
such probable place of habitation was the mesa and slopes known
by American pioneers as Indian Flat and later named Linda
Vista by the son of its first non-native settler. This site, close to
the waters of the Arroyo Seco, must have proven a convenient
campground and lookout place for the Indians.

The Franciscan padres brought with them conversion for the
Indians, as well as grapes and oranges for planting. Some of the
natives located around the Mission San Gabriel objected to the
confinement and enforced labor that went along with conversion,
and they escaped to the nearby rugged San Gabriels. The Arroyo
Seco was one of the natural routes for them to use and the slopes

and ravines of Linda Vista, convenient places to pause for rest or concealment.

The padres' plans for the Indians ultimately failed, and within little more than 100 years after the Spaniards' arrival, practically all evidence had disappeared from southern California of the original natives.

What references to Gabrieliños support the Linda Vista area's name of Indian Flat? Hiram Reid (not to be confused with Hugo Reid, an early annalist of the Gabrieliños) notes in his 1895 history of Pasadena that "Even as late as 1884-1885, the fine body of land now known as Linda Vista was called 'Indian Flat' because it had been for many years occupied by one of these fragmental Indian settlements."[1]

Al Carr, son of Pasadena pioneers Ezra and Jeanne Carr, wrote contemporary accounts of the Arroyo of the 1870s and the 1880s, noting:

> All of the east and west streets led into the Arroyo Seco, then segregated into wood lots by rough, steep grades, there being two from Colorado Street, one leading south and one north to the mesa known as Indian Flat, an old Indian rancheria site later called Linda Vista.[2]

Finally, noted Gabrielino authority Bernice Eastman Johnston underscores the fact of Indians in the Linda Vista area when she comments in the Southwest Museum *Masterkey* on relics, mostly cooking implements, dug up during an excavation:

> Tradition places a group [of Gabrieliños]. . . along the Linda Vista palisades to the west. A concentration of Indian material was found here, south of Lida Street and on the grounds of the grammar school [Linda Vista School] nearby.[3]

During the early mission days, Corporal José María Verdugo, once a leather-jacket soldier at the San Diego Presidio, concluded his military career at the Mission San Gabriel Archangel, where he had arrived in the founding year of 1771. In the early days, while marching through the countryside as a king's soldier, he undoubtedly relished the natural beauty of the place and realized its potential. Later, to earn extra money, he herded cattle on certain of the area's unoccupied territory, and after he married Encarnación Lopez in 1779, he began to want land of his own where he could graze his cattle and where he could establish a family homestead.

In 1784 Verdugo and fellow soldiers Juan José Dominguez and Manuel Nieto, all anticipating retirement and apparently acting together, asked for permission to place their cattle and horses in areas near Los Angeles. The soldiers hoped to be rewarded for years of faithful military service. Military commander and Alta California Governor Pedro Fages granted the three men's requests and awarded them vast grazing permits.

Fages' response to Verdugo's petition reads:

> I concede to the petitioner the permission which he solicits to keep his cattle and horses at the 'Arroyo Hondo' [the Arroyo Seco]...provided that he does not prejudice the... Mission, nor the inhabitants of the Reina de Los Angeles, and having some one in charge, without being exposed to the gentile Indians, nor in any manner injuring them.[4]

On October 10, 1784, Verdugo received his grazing permit to 36,000 acres of land, located primarily in what are now Glendale and large parts of Burbank. The land was then known as La Zanja, meaning water ditch, because of the prevalence of water within its boundaries. Within a few years Verdugo, a devout Catholic, officially named the rancho San Rafael, after one of the seven angels said to stand by the throne of God.

Although Verdugo's permit was the smallest of the three 1784 Spanish grazing tracts (Dominguez's and Nieto's requests were also granted), Rancho San Rafael was still an enviable portion. A triangular wedge of rough, hilly land, the rancho separated the San Gabriel and San Fernando valleys, with the Los Angeles River defining the western boundary, the San Gabriel Mountains the northern boundary, and the Arroyo Seco the eastern boundary. Today, a drive along the freeways that crisscross the land reveals the rancho's awesome proportions and the work it must have taken vaqueros to oversee its chaparral-covered hills and steep, twisting canyons.

When Verdugo received his land, his permit stipulated not only the grazing of cattle but also the herding of sheep. A further regulation prohibited the killing of female horses. Rancho animals were branded with the rancho's insignia—"S slant-bar S." This same mark is part of the coat-of-arms of Occidental College, built on lands once belonging to Rancho San Rafael.[5]

Verdugo was made captain of the guard at San Gabriel the same year that he was given grazing rights. He did not ask for permission to move immediately onto his land because of obligations he still had at the mission, so one of his brothers lived on the rancho, tending it and building a hut made of branches and twigs, much like the Gabrieliño dwellings. Verdugo, in the meantime, grew anxious when he heard rumors that a new mission might be established on the site of Rancho San Rafael. If this occurred, his permit would be revoked. However, in 1797 the mission, named Mission San Fernando, was located at Francisco

One of the several Verdugo adobes built in the Glendale area. Photo dates from 1857.

Reyes' Rancho Encino. Verdugo was then able to celebrate the permanency of his claim.

No longer threatened with losing his rancho, Verdugo, in ill health, asked for authorization to retire from the military, move his family to Rancho San Rafael and build an adobe. Regulations required a retired and infirm soldier to live in a pueblo, but Verdugo argued that if he lived in Los Angeles, he would be subjected to the numerous "fatigues" of close contact with others. His particular illness required "greater ease."[6] Not only was he given permission to settle on the rancho, but he also received a confirmation of his grant. This confirmation commended him for increasing the numbers of his cattle, building an irrigation system and planting crops.

Even though material luxuries were few during the early years at Rancho San Rafael, life there was pleasant for the Verdugos. Indian servants did much of the labor, and numerous Verdugo relatives lived throughout the California province and visited frequently. Furthermore, Verdugo's name generated respect in Los Angeles, and his brother, Mariano de la Luz Verdugo, served as the third *alcalde* (mayor) of the pueblo.

Though never totally regaining his health, Verdugo enjoyed the many visitors that arrived at the rancho. Tables were laden with ranch-grown fruits and vegetables, and meat came from the rancho herds. Fiestas, family weddings, cock-fights, bull-fights and horse races held on the property provided entertainment for the guests.

In his book *Cattle on a Thousand Hills,* Robert Glass Cleland gives the circumstances of José María Verdugo's 1832 death: "dropsy, old age, frequent bleedings, and perhaps high blood pressure aggravated by a choleric temper."[7] In his will Verdugo left a huge, debt-free estate. His unmarried daughter, Catalina, and his son, Julio (about forty at the time and married to María de Jésus Romero), were left all of the rancho properties. María Josefa and María Ignacio, Verdugo's two married daughters, were disappointed when they only received various livestock, and they unsuccessfully protested being left no land.

The sole male heir, Julio Verdugo, now a cattle baron, busied himself with supervising the work of the rancho and building new adobes for his own growing family; he is reported to have had as many as eleven sons. Accompanied by at least one of these sons, he frequently rode horseback into Los Angeles, revelling in his role of *juez de campo* (judge of the countryside) of rodeos held on the rancho, and often wearing the colorful costume of a Spanish *caballero*. He also looked out for Catalina, who spent most of her days with nephews, especially Teodoro.

Rancho San Rafael suffered little effect when Mexico gained its independence from Spain in 1821 or when the Mexican government secularized the missions in the early 1830s and Indians living on the mission lands were dispersed. Times were good to the Verdugo family, even during these years of historic change and turmoil.

A setback finally occurred in 1843 when the Verdugos lost the northern foothill regions of their rancho to Ignacio Coronel, secretary of the Los Angeles *ayuntamiento* (city council). Coronel, on a trip to the Tujunga region, had spotted what appeared to be vacant land. Deciding this would be an ideal place for a family ranch and home, he petitioned Governor Manuel Micheltorena for the land, submitting a map of the boundaries, which included the water-rich Linda Vista area. Verdugo appealed to the governor not to grant the petition, yet argue as he might that the land was part of his rancho, his pleas were ignored. On May 14, 1843, La Cañada atras de Los Berdugos ("the glen behind the Berdugos"— Verdugo was often spelled Berdugo) was granted to Coronel.

Members of the Coronel family lived on the La Cañada rancho for several years. But when bands of ex-neophyte Indians began galloping down the La Cañada Valley from their hideouts in the mountains, making periodic horse-stealing forays on local ranches, Coronel decided it was time for the family to return to Los Angeles.

Since Coronel was a prominent member of the Los Angeles community, busy with pueblo matters and with little time to spare on the neglected La Cañada property, he sold it to a man

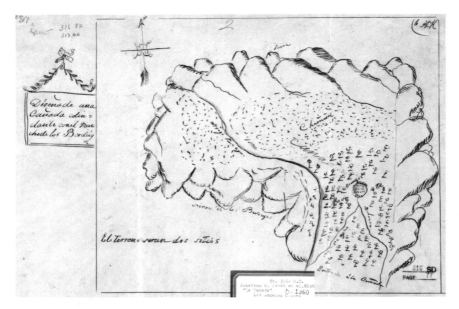

Diseño of Rancho La Cañada. *Courtesy Bancroft Library, University of California, Berkeley.*

named Borie who was connected with the shipping business. When the man died, ownership reverted to Coronel. In 1852 Coronel sold the rancho again, this time to two young law partners from the East, Jonathan Scott and Benjamin Hayes. Scott soon bought Hayes' interest for $2,500.[8]

After the Mexican-American War, the new United States government in 1851 appointed a special commission to investigate land titles in order to clear up vague land ownership claims in California. In actuality, the laws and financial practices of the United States were so unfamiliar to the Mexican populace, that the landowners never adequately understood their ownership rights.

That same year Julio Verdugo and Catalina petitioned the courts to settle claims that had been made against their land. Attorney Joseph Lancaster Brent, who had arrived a year earlier from Maryland, represented them. Brent obtained confirmation

Joseph Lancaster Brent, Julio
Verdugo's legal counsel.

of Julio's title in 1855 and purchased for himself 671 acres of the
rancho along the Los Angeles River. He also bought 800 acres of
Rancho San Pasqual's Marengo Tract, located in what is now a
part of South Pasadena.

Brent wrote of his early experiences with California legal
matters:

> The great political influence I had acquired came from my
> control over the California population, most of whom were
> my clients, and who, ignorant of American politics, always
> followed my recommendations. An old man named Verdugo
> [Julio], a client of mine, took great pride upon each election
> day, in riding up to me accompanied by ten of his sons and
> sons-in-law, and demanding from me tickets to be voted at
> the election by his whole clan.[9]

Julio Verdugo had never ceased wanting to gain back the land
of Linda Vista and the Arroyo, and since Scott desired land on
which to grow grain, in 1858 Scott traded the Rancho de la
Sierra de los Berdugos to Julio for part of the Rancho San Rafael
now included in Burbank. Once again Linda Vista belonged to

the Verdugos! Julio and Catalina then divided the rancho, with the sister receiving the northern portion, including Linda Vista. But no legal records were made of the division.

Verdugo's problems, however, were far from over. Three years after his trade with Scott, Julio mortgaged his and Catalina's property to Jacob Elias, a Los Angeles merchant. Verdugo needed to buy seed, order supplies, pay taxes and enlarge the Verdugo adobe, located in what is now Glendale. The terms of the mortgage were 3% interest a month, which compounded to over 40% a year. Verdugo, unsophisticated about United States laws and business methods, watched helplessly as interest and taxes spiraled. As if this were not enough, havoc was created in the cattle industry by the drought of the 1860s. Bodies of cattle, casualties of starvation and thirst, littered the Verdugo rancho.

With their herds perishing, the Verdugos found themselves unable to meet the mounting costs of mortgage payments and legal fees. They desperately needed the services of Brent again, but he was serving as a brigadier-general with the Confederates in the Civil War and could no longer offer the bankrupt brother and sister legal assistance.[10] Foreclosure proceedings were finally brought against Julio and Catalina.

The courts acted accordingly, confiscating Verdugo property and ordering an official survey in 1869. A group of men headed by Alfred Beck Chapman, a Los Angeles lawyer later to become district attorney, presented the highest bid at an auction for the land.

Chapman's three partners were Andrew Glassell, who eventually owned parcels of land east of present-day Griffith Park; Prudent Beaudry of Los Angeles; and O.W. Childs, who was deeded prime land by Chapman that became the Childs Tract in Glendale. Wanting to clear up title to the rancho lands, the syndicate sued 36 defendants, many of them Verdugo relatives or persons married to Verdugo family members and to whom Julio Verdugo had either sold or given parcels. All of the defendants, the plaintiffs claimed, were living on land not legally determined as theirs.

Alfred Beck Chapman received
Verdugo land from foreclosure
proceedings and sold to
Benjamin Dreyfus.

O.W. Childs, owner of the
sprawling Childs Tract in
what is now a part of Glendale.

The legal suit resulted in "The Great Partition of 1871," one of the most famous land trials in southern California. The court decreed that the rancho should be partitioned into 31 parts among 28 persons. Not wanting to leave Julio homeless, Chapman quit-claimed 200 acres to the aging man, including his adobe. Other family members received various parcels.

In 1871 Benjamin Dreyfus, an investor from Anaheim, bought the largest section of Rancho San Rafael. His parcel reached from the Eagle Rock area to Linda Vista. Prudent Beaudry bought Pasadena's San Rafael section, land south of Linda Vista and running along the Arroyo Seco across from South Pasadena.

Catalina, who had been blinded by smallpox, was allowed to remain in her Verdugo Canyon adobe with her nephew, Teodoro, and there she died in that same year. Julio died in 1876. Both were in their 80s. Ironically, a patent of Rancho San Rafael, spelling out the vague boundaries of the past century, was not issued until 1882. Though the titles had been confirmed much earlier, issuance of the patent had been tied up for years in the overcrowded courts.

Describing the loss of a historic California ranch, W.W. Robinson wrote in his introduction to *Maps of Los Angeles:*

> When the referees and surveyors had completed, in 1871, the partitioning of Rancho San Rafael...the Verdugo rancho was no more. And what was left to members of the Verdugo family...would presently melt before the invasion of creditors and newcomers. All but two of the Verdugo adobe homes that once dotted the great 36,000 acre rancho sank into ruin and oblivion.[11]

Rancho San Rafael's original family, however, lives on today in such names as Verdugo Canyon, Verdugo City, and Verdugo Boulevard.

Moses Langley Wicks, c. 1880,
sold Linda Vista property to
John Yocum.

Chapter Two

A Prelude and a Boom, 1871-1887

> The present Linda Vista was a remote, uninviting tract of wild land in 1883 when one J.D. Yocum purchased it. Heavily wooded with live oak and densely covered with greasewood and chapparal [sic], this charming section of the present city had then only a few native Mexican families living in what had long been known as "Indian Flat."
>
> Harold D. Carew,
> *Pasadena* (1930).

An enterprising Benjamin Dreyfus arrived in Anaheim in 1860, one of a group of German immigrants who came to California in the mid-nineteenth century. The 35-year old Dreyfus was ambitious and eager to leave his mark on the frontier. Accordingly, he eventually not only served as mayor of the city, but he ran a store, bred horses, grew grapes, made wine, and bought and sold real estate. His letters reveal a light-hearted spirit. In one he commented, "Wine will be clear if you say three times Ave Maria purisima and take a drink afterwards." Another stated, "Keep your feet warm and your head cool which is also very essential in wine making." He might close a letter with a pseudo-Spanish flourish, "Muchas salutas a todas," and send rose cuttings to the recipient.[1]

Dreyfus, who thrived on new business ventures, started raising sheep on his Eagle Rock and Linda Vista property. In 1883 he sold the land as vineyard plots to a real estate syndicate headed by Moses Langley Wicks of Anaheim. Dreyfus insisted on keeping the mineral rights, which he later sold to James De Barth Shorb, an early developer of Pasadena and San Marino. Dreyfus died in 1886 at the age of 61 after a life in which he played a major role in both the blossoming of Anaheim and the development of Arroyo surroundings.

During the years that Dreyfus owned Rancho San Rafael property, squatters wandered to the Linda Vista area. But as newcomers from the East and Midwest settled in the area, attracted by the climate, soil and setting, these squatters drifted away.

Moses Wicks was an austere, "smooth speaking" "gentleman of vision" from Mississippi. As a newcomer to southern California, he went first to Anaheim, where he opened a law office, and then to Los Angeles, where his interests became more focused on real estate speculation.[2] Wicks formed a syndicate that included Charley Watts, a Pasadena resident and investor who arrived from Chicago in 1874; E.T. Wright, onetime county surveyor; and H. Hodgkins, a "retired capitalist of Los Angeles, lured out of retirement by the prospects of fortune getting."[3] These four men cannily anticipated the growth of the Southland, buying up great amounts of property, especially in the Glendale area, and quickly converting stock range into tillable land, sometimes selling parcels for sizable gains within six months of their purchase. After buying the northeast section of Rancho San Rafael from Dreyfus in the spring of 1883, the summer and fall of that same year they sold Linda Vista portions to Pasadenan John DeWeese Yocum.

John D. Yocum and his wife, Hannah, came to southern California from Iowa in 1882 for undoubtedly the same reason as many other midwestern Quakers. Rural people, they saw "the promise of rich, new soil waiting to be cultivated and planted."[4] Pasadena with its yielding orchards and year-round temperate climate was a favored location, and these farmers adapted their wheat-growing skills to citrus-growing ones.

Born in 1833, John was the son of Quakers Samuel and Jane. Hannah was the daughter of Quakers Nathan P. and Lydia Grissell. The Yocums were married in Belmont County, Ohio, in 1857 but moved to Iowa before coming to California. John and Hannah's only child, Nathan Grissell Yocum, was born in Belmont County on November 4, 1862. Nathan and his wife, Lydia, childless in 1882, accompanied his parents to California.

The Yocums moved onto four acres on Pasadena's Monk Hill. Los Angeles County Hall of Records ledgers list the sale date as May 22, 1882. John Yocum bought the property for $325 gold coin from two other Iowa Quakers, John H. Painter and Benjamin F. Ball, who owned a huge 2,000-acre tract in north Pasadena.[5]

Monk Hill looks across the Arroyo to Linda Vista, and from his home on Marengo Avenue, John Yocum could see the vacant, untamed, western slopes. He knew the land was for sale and thought the location an ideal spot to start his own farm. Following in the Quaker tradition, Yocum longed for neighborhood and fellowship, and he could found a small community there on the bluffs overlooking Pasadena. He could also engage in some real estate speculation.

Including Nathan in all of his plans, Yocum sold for a sizable profit a portion of his Marengo Avenue property along with a tract he owned on nearby Mountain and Wilson streets. The Yocums then used the sale proceeds to buy up the entire Linda Vista hillside, acquiring the Watts Tract from the Wicks syndicate. In addition they secured other hillside lands from Shorb's Lake Vineyard Land and Water Association as well as Shorb family property on the Arroyo bottom, listing this latter purchase in the name of Hannah. The Yocums now dominated all of Linda Vista,

> from the front of Jumbo Knob opposite Reservoir Hill up to the Verdugo hills near Devil's Gate, and comprised of arroyo bottom and bluff lands, mesa land and mountain land, all densely covered with greasewood and other native chap.[6]

Jumbo Knob is the hill that looms over the Arroyo on the west side of the Linda Vista Bridge. The hill forms the curve where Linda Vista Avenue changes directions from south to west. This particular chunk of jutting terrain was so-called because when viewed from certain angles, it resembled the head of Barnum's elephant, the trunk reaching down into the Arroyo's waters.

Because of subsequent excavations, this likeness is mainly to be imagined today.

Anxious to establish themselves and lay down roots, the Yocums built a two-story farmhouse on a hill west of the Arroyo and below where the Flintridge Academy now stands, on land north of what is now Lida Street. Three years later John and Hannah moved to a new home built closer to Devil's Gate Dam, Nathan and Lydia remaining in the original house. Both homes had wide verandas and views across the Arroyo. Hearsay has it that Nathan coined the community's name by looking out over the slopes and saying with awe, "Linda vista!" [Pretty view]. The Yocum houses were torn down in the 1920s.

For the first several years in Linda Vista, father and son worked vigorously on their property, using the help of men who lived in the new community or who traveled in from Pasadena as day-laborers. These men cleared, leveled and tilled the soil and put an area aside for fruit drying. They drove tunnels into hillsides to obtain water and planted 12,000 peach and apricot trees south of the Yocum homes. Finally, they developed certain property into marketable ranch and home sites and began to sell parcels. The Los Angeles *Evening Express* commented in 1886 on the Yocum project:

> From Monk's hill the view is grand. Across the valley is "Indian Flat," a little nook of eleven hundred acres in the Verdugo Mountains, owned by Mr. Yocum, who made it valuable by driving six tunnels into the mountains, and getting all the water he needed.[7]

The Yocums earned a reputation for hospitality, much in the tradition of the early rancheros. Comfortable rooms were made available for newly arrived settlers waiting to find places to live, and hearty meals were stretched to feed unexpected guests. Naturalist John Muir reportedly visited the Yocums during one of his frequent trips from Yosemite to be with his Pasadena friends, Jeanne and Ezra Carr and O.H. Congar.[8]

Other settlers instrumental in Linda Vista's growth soon joined the Yocums. Byron Clark, a lover of horticulture and new

This older photo shows a lush and woodsy Arroyo. Oldtimers frequently described it this way.

enterprises, figured prominently in the community's future. His gardening efforts began in the 1870s in Anaheim, and in 1882 he moved to eleven acres on Monk Hill at Marengo Avenue and Villa

Street, where he was a neighbor of the Yocums. At this time, while Yocum was busy buying up Linda Vista, Clark purchased acreage for blackberry plants in the Arroyo. He also wanted to try tree farming and moved north of Pasadena with his wife and two daughters to a forty-acre tract, which he named Altadena (above Pasadena).

Clark's move to Altadena was a leap into foothill-development activities. The Woodbury brothers of Pasadena named him a director of their California Olive Company, which held 200 acres adjacent to Clark's land. Clark oversaw the planting of the company's olive trees and supervised the building of its irrigation system, including a dam above Millard Canyon and pipes leading to the orchard. The business' goal was to process and sell olive oil, but the drought of 1886, combined with real estate over-extensions of the principals involved, left no money for the processing plant, and the company was liquidated.[9] The olive trees were sold and removed to new sites, and the land was turned into the Woodbury Subdivision. The dam and pipes were taken over by the Millard Canyon Water Company, of which Clark was also a director, to supply water to the subdivision. Clark now decided to go into the nursery business and about 1886 moved to vacant land in Linda Vista. He gave permission for the use of the Altadena name for the Woodbury development.

Clark's pride was the family house he built at the intersection of present-day Linda Vista Avenue and Inverness Drive. (Present-day Inverness Drive was first named Clark Street.) The home had a rock foundation, with windows and porches facing south. Clark immediately started to do what he loved best—experiment with new plantings. He lined both sides of the driveway with banana trees and placed rose bushes, at that time an ecological wonder, in the front yard. A cow in the backyard munched alfalfa.[10]

Yocum and L.G. Kellogg, Clark's brother-in-law from Anaheim, joined Clark in buying twenty acres of land for the Park Nursery Company on Park Avenue (now named Linda Vista Avenue). This land extended west of the avenue and on both sides of Inverness Drive. The three men served as directors and officers, and showrooms were located in Pasadena at the corner of Colorado Street and Pasadena Avenue. Hothouses and nursery yards, with palms and flowers growing in profusion, appeared south of Clark's home.

The Pasadena *Daily Union* noted the area's new nursery:

> Many seem to think a nursery an unnecessary adjunct in this clime. . . . But there are many plants, trees and shrubs that need cultivation, transplanting, etc., and many that are not common here. These, of course, make necessary an institution. . . . Pasadena has such a place in the Park Nursery, which is composed of twenty acres of the finest land in the San Gabriel Valley, located on the west side of the Arroyo Seco, in what is commonly known as the Yocum tract. At this nursery they have three large and commodious houses and one large hothouse. . . . There is, perhaps, not a rose known to the botanist which this nursery does not already have or is not making efforts to introduce.[11]

Ever anxious to test new horticultural varieties, Clark made numerous horse-and-buggy trips to Santa Barbara to collect specimens, often taking along his family. He also acted as chief salesman for the nursery. In one ten-day period, he sold 1,000 pepper trees, which were planted in surrounding San Gabriel Valley neighborhoods.[12]

James A. Riggins, local businessman, and Clark started a fruit crystallization plant in 1886. The two men put up a building on Glenarm Street in Pasadena, but the venture failed to make a profit and work had to be suspended.

Clark's most enduring reputation is as an early beautifier of the Pasadena landscape. According to historian J.W. Wood:

> [Clark] stimulated the embellishment of many homes in Pasadena with new and heretofore untried varieties of trees and plants. Many fine old trees now growing in Pasadena streets and grounds were planted there by him or by his advice.[13]

As early as 1887, the new city of Pasadena buzzed about

Looking west across the Arroyo to Jumbo Knob, c. 1900.

"taking in" Linda Vista, concerned that the area might degenerate. A local paper proclaimed:

> A timely suggestion is made in extending the city limits, that they include the Arroyo Seco and a considerable portion of the hills on the other side of the Arroyo. If this is not done we are more than likely to have that now secluded and picturesque canyon turned into a resort for saloons and disreputable homes.[14]

That same year, perhaps not by coincidence, Yocum and Clark founded the Linda Vista Land and Improvement Association. Charter members included L.G. Kellogg, H.T. Sanborn and S.B. Smith. The group started with $200,000 capital stock and $140,000 subscription money, which they immediately put to use for school and water projects.[15]

The association also built the Linda Vista Hotel, a twelve-room combination hostelry and boarding house at the corner of what was then Park Avenue and Clark Street, but the structure served more as a home for area workers than for visitors. It was also used as a community recreation center, and Sunday dinners were served to guests who might arrive by horse and buggy or by bicycle. Within the next few years, the hotel changed management several times. When a certain Mrs. Griggs was proprietor, she called the hotel the "Pepper Pot," because of the many pepper trees surrounding it. Robert Carson, a good friend of Yocum's, ran the place next under the name of the Carson Hotel. In 1903 George Pierson was the last owner of record.

The Linda Vista Land and Improvement Association needed ingenuity to exploit the area's existing water resources, and they relied heavily on Clark's hydraulic experiences in Altadena. One water system was installed by digging a tunnel at the top of Wildcat Canyon, a rugged ravine behind Yocum's home, to tap underground springs. Dr. Jacob Hodge, a recent arrival to Linda Vista, reacted to work done on his property: "There is a well on it ten feet deep which yields water not less than two feet in depth even in the driest time of the year"[16] The community worried about the Shorb Company's plans to dig a series of seven-by-eight-foot tunnels in local hills, including Linda Vista's, to divert water to a Los Angeles reservoir. The idea met with strong local opposition and was never carried out.[17]

The Land and Improvement Association also laid out the area's original dirt roads. Through the years street names have reflected the times: Belmont Drive (now Parkview Avenue) for the Yocum's native Ohio county; Clark Street (now Inverness Drive) after Byron Clark; Park Avenue (changed to Linda Vista Avenue in 1919) after Clark's nursery; Lida Street after Yocum's daughter-in-law, Lydia; Hancock Avenue for an early county surveyor (later named West Avenue and then Wellington Avenue in 1930 after the Chicago street where the Richards family lived before building what is now Pegfair); Mundell Avenue (now Ontario Avenue) after a business partner of the Yocums; Villa Court (no longer there, but approximately where La Vista Place is now) for the new Italianate influence being introduced to

Pasadena by author Grace Ellery Channing and other area new-comers; Myrtle Street for the wife of J.M. Jensen, a tract developer of the 1910-1920 decade; and Avalon Avenue for the popular vacation village on Catalina Island.

With his Linda Vista responsibilities well in hand, Yocum (who referred to himself as "Professor," saying he had taught at Piney College in Iowa and Berea College in Kentucky) partici-pated in Pasadena community affairs. He was a member of the boards of Throop Polytechnic Institute, the Pasadena Board of Trade and the First Universalist Church. Both John and Nathan actively supported local temperance activities.

Nathan was in his early twenties when the family arrived in Pasadena. An outgoing and energetic young man, his enthusiasm spread to all his affairs. An incident revealing his nature occurred in 1886 when he befriended a Los Angeles *Express* reporter on a railroad ride from Los Angeles to Pasadena. The anonymous newspaperman wrote that he had taken

> cars of the Los Angeles and San Gabriel Valley railroad bound for the terminus,...to get a bit of fresh air, a drink of pure water, and smell the ground, with its grasses and beautiful flowers, to listen to the songs of the wild birds, to gaze upon the sublime scenery of mountain and vale....On the train we had the plea-sure of meeting N.G. Yocum and his amiable wife, who, in learning our desire to see as much as possible, offered to pro-cure a team, and do the honors of the occasion, an invitation which was accepted with pleasure.[18]

Panoramic views of Linda Vista were part of the excursion.

These were the days of the Southland's famous real estate boom. Distances suddenly meant less as railway tracks began to extend through southern California, connecting townsites served by the Santa Fe Railroad Company. In 1886 the Santa Fe and Southern Pacific railways battled in a price war for transconti-nental passengers, and one-way tickets from the East were only $25, sometimes cheaper. Travelers responded accordingly.

As opportunistic real estate agents poured into southern California from San Francisco, Chicago and New York, large numbers of people also arrived, many eager to buy property. The boom of 1886-1888 was on, and Pasadena shared heartily in the pandemonium. Orange groves were cut up into town lots. A broker simply nailed a notice on his door announcing property for sale and buyers came knocking. John Yocum, who from his first days in Pasadena had eagerly participated in land ventures, now bought, sold and traded with added zest.

Nathan, enthusiastic by nature, caught the real estate fever from his father. Moses Wicks and his partner Charlie Watts, who had sold John Yocum Linda Vista land, were undoubtedly another influence on Nathan at that time. Nathan must have been impressed by the youth of these entrepreneurs, and here he was, only in his mid-twenties.

With his father as an underwriter, Nathan formed a syndicate of influential men: I.N. Mundell, one of the original settlers of Pasadena's Indiana Colony, who once served as city marshal; H. W. Ogden, who later moved to Louisiana where he was in the state House of Representatives; and Thomas F. Flynn, a successful Pasadena businessman who promoted San Diego County's Linda Rosa community, heavily advertised in Pasadena papers of the day. These men referred to their organization as the Pasadena Park Tract Land and Water Company.

In October 1887 the syndicate bought 600 acres of Linda Vista land for $40,000 from John Yocum.[19] At this time the slopes became known as "lower" and "upper" Linda Vista. (The 600 acres located in the southern end around Jumbo Knob were considered the lower portion.) The business also purchased from a man named Silbey 52 acres on Pasadena's Reservoir Hill, which overlooked the Arroyo, and developed it into the Park Place Tract, advertising lots as outstanding sites for gracious homes. (Reservoir Hill is the area northeast of the Linda Vista Bridge and above Brookside Park.

The Park Place Improvement Company was formed to manage the tract. With Mundell as president, the company's office was at 28 Colorado Street in Pasadena. Like Wicks and other developers of the day, Nathan and his partners installed a horse-drawn railway around the streets of their tract to make the property more saleable. Known as the West Pasadena Railway, the tracks stretched from Colorado Boulevard and Fair Oaks Avenue west to the Park Place tract. From there they wound through the subdivision, crossed the Arroyo on a bridge where the Linda Vista Bridge (often referred to presently as the Holly Street Bridge) now stands, and headed north to Park Place Nursery.

The bridge over the Arroyo was John Yocum's project. The impressive structure had two 120-foot spans, one 140-foot span, and an 18-foot roadway. It cost the development company $8,000. Cars and horses were housed in barns behind the Linda Vista Hotel.

The railway shuttled interested buyers through the Park Place lots and also provided Linda Vista residents with a ride to

Looking west across the Arroyo to Linda Vista, c. 1900.

and from Pasadena for shopping and business. The local paper extolled the railway's virtues:

> The Park Place cars were crowded with tourists yesterday who rode out to the end of the line to see the beautiful Park Place Nursery. The track is in excellent condition, the cars are easy riders, and on the whole, a ride over this route is as much enjoyed as a carriage ride.[20]

Emile Heseldon Philbrook, a drawing teacher recently arrived in Pasadena, recalled riding the railway:

> I arrived May 19, 1888, just a few days after the incorporation of the West Pasadena Railway Company, and it consisted of a single tract in West Pasadena, two open cars and eight miles, and, oh, how wet the passengers could be when riding on those cars in a mountain downpour. Just as wet as dusty when walking in dry weather.[21]

Nathan's syndicate, with the participation of John Yocum, next invested in property located west of Lake Elsinore in San Diego County. The idea was to create out of wasteland a new and thriving city named Lucerne (not the present Lucerne Valley). The consideration paid was $145,000, and the Pasadena *Daily Union* announced that the property should be worth half a million dollars after it was subdivided.[22]

Numerous articles touted Lucerne's potential for coal mining, farming and population growth, and advertisements in the Pasadena paper described the development in superlatives:

> Lucerne excells all other townsites in Southern California ....Nature has evidently planned for a manufacturing center...Lucerne is supplied with an abundance of PURE MOUNTAIN WATER sufficient for all purposes.[23]

In a local Pasadena history manuscript, pioneer T.D. Allin stated, "Nate Yocum, from Pasadena, another product of Iowa, laid out a tract west of the lake [Elsinore] and named it Lucerne." He goes on to describe Nathan's and another real estate salesman's abilities:

> Frank Heald and Nate Yocum were the greatest boosters and land boomers I have ever known. In later years we have

had schools of salesmanship, and have trained men in salesmanship, but Frank Heald and Nate Yocum, without such
training, could sell anything, and would have made our later
salesmen look like amateurs in comparison.[24]

Families continued to arrive in Linda Vista, developing farms
on large tracts. In 1888 the Chamberlains moved to approximately
200 acres and built a ranch house where the Pegfair estate now
stands. The property extended west to the summit of the San
Rafael Hills, east to the Arroyo and south to Salvia Canyon. Here
the owners planted peach trees and maintained the orchards
until they sold the property to Marshall D. Fiscus in 1907.

Visionary Dr. Jacob Hodge came to Linda Vista in 1888,
purchasing 45 acres from Yocum in the northwest area and
building a canyon home and a twelve-foot wide road to the
1800-foot summit at the back of his land. For additional water, he
erected a reservoir and windmill connected by pipes to a canyon
well, but the windmill toppled during a destructive 1891 wind
storm. Hodge's intent was not only to have a farm but also to
establish a sanitarium for his patients who were recovering
from tuberculosis.

With his windmill destroyed, Hodge abandoned his plans for
a Linda Vista sanitarium. Instead, in 1895 in rooms rented from
the Masonic Temple at Colorado Boulevard and Raymond Avenue,
he opened the Receiving Hospital and Surgical Institute, the first
regular hospital in Pasadena. Later that year, he operated another
receiving hospital in the upper two floors of a building on the
northwest corner of Raymond Avenue and Green Street, but the
hospital business interefered with his private practice, and he
left the project. This same hospital changed hands several times,
and the venture was finally relocated to Fairmont Avenue and
Congress Street, where it evolved into the Huntington Memorial
Hospital.

Development was also going on in the Arroyo area below
Linda Vista. James W. Scoville, one of the wealthiest early Pasadena pioneers, built an Italian-style villa on his seventeen-acre
estate that extended in the Arroyo from Orange Grove Boulevard
near the Carr's Carmelita home to Jumbo Knob.

Looking west across the Arroyo to upper Linda Vista, c. 1900.

From 1887 to 1889 Scoville and his son, Charles Burton Scoville, graded extensively in the Arroyo and surrounding slopes, consequently altering the original terrain of that portion of Linda Vista. They built a dam that created an artificial lake just south of where the Linda Vista Bridge now stands. A tall pump house loomed up from the landscape. Above the dam on the western slope, the Scovilles built a shooting lodge of river rock for marksmanship competitions. During the hard times following the real estate collapse, unemployed area men were hired to put up retaining walls around these structures.

Scoville also constructed a bridge that connected Arroyo Drive with the country road that approximates today's Colorado Boulevard leading to Glendale. The eighty-foot timber-truss span was the only one over the Arroyo leading directly into the pass that heads west and goes by the Eagle Rock. But even with this bridge, travel between Pasadena and Glendale was tedious. A better way to cross the Arroyo was needed, so in 1913 Pasadena built the Colorado Street bridge, a 1,500-foot span.

As Pasadena grew, Linda Vista and the Arroyo became favorite outing spots. Visitors came to this rural area for hikes, picnics, hayrides and camp-outs. Bird-egg collecting was a favorite activity. For the equestrian, a horseback riding trail stretched from Pasadena west through the ranches and hills of Linda Vista. This trail was euphemistically called the "Ladies Trail" because a woman could ride to the top without being exposed to any unnecessary danger. As the horse made its way to the crest of Linda Vista peak, the rider might catch a glimpse of old gold-mining efforts, for the Linda Vista area had mineral content and miners had been there.

The Arroyo, scene of youthful adventures, was described with Tom Sawyer charm in a manuscript by Al Carr, son of Ezra and Jeanne Carr. Carr was part of a spirited group of young men from Pasadena that held "wildcat hunts" in the Arroyo, especially near heavily wooded Linda Vista. Besides Carr, the group included Charlie Watts, Wicks' partner and one-time owner of a section of Linda Vista; Arturo Bandini, an ardent hunter and scion of an old Californio family; Whitt Elliott, son of the first president of the Indiana Colony and whose sister married Arturo Bandini; and Charlie Winston, a popular young Pasadenan. At early morning these young men saddled their horses and followed a pack of dogs, usually greyhounds, to chase lynx and fox up toward Linda Vista. If the prey was a cat, once it was treed, the dogs circled below and one of the hunters "shinned" up the tree and, according to Carr, "jabbed the snarling cat on the end farthest removed from the snarl, the cat leaped and landed in a swirl of dogs who emerged from the kill with many souvenirs of the fray but eager for the next encounter."[25]

In those days horse-drawn buggies traveled over Yocum's bridge, bringing visitors to the picturesque village. The horses trotted down one-laned Park Avenue, newly planted on either side with Byron Clark's pepper trees. Occasional farm houses appeared, set back from the roads amid well-tended fields and orchards. From porches and pathways residents might wave at the visitor. The community was friendly, open and welcoming.

CHAPTER THREE

After the Boom

One evening a very long time ago, Professor Yocum stood on the hill in front of his home, holding the hand of a little friend. As he looked away to the hills and the valley below, he made a very prophetic remark: "Childie, I see homes and roads covering this valley and reaching to the very tops of yonder hills." He said "homes," not "houses," and let us hope that everyone who comes to live in his valley or upon his hillsides will build a "home," not just a house.

Blanche Dorn,
Unpublished manuscript (1978).

Not even a railway running through Park Place could assure the tract's success. Nathan Yocum and his partners had been carried along by high hopes generated at the peak of the real estate craze. When the boom collapsed, so did their financial situation.

San Gabriel Valley historian Harold D. Carew comments about the times:

While the land-gambling mania was on, many of the large tracts were cut up into lots, and those who were able to unload these holdings were made wealthy. Those who bought at peak prices were left high and dry when the "boom" started on the tobaggan in 1889, and could not sell at any price. The year 1890 was a dismal time; business picked up slightly for a year or two, and then came the panic of 1893, which left real estate owners in a worse plight than they had been in when the prices collapsed. Thousands and thousands of dollars were lost by investors who hoped to profit handsomely, and the scenes of frenzy and excitement were shifted to the bankruptcy courts.[1]

Mortgages went on record at a furious rate with obligations far exceeding cash. When banks began to refuse the financing of future deals in city subdivisions or rural townsites, indebtedness became rampant. Interest rates, which had been at 6%, climbed to as high as 13%. According to one southern California historian, "... people who had boasted of the huge amounts of money involved in boom transactions now became aware that paper profits, and not liquid capital, had been the lifeblood of the flurry."[2]

Nathan developed financial problems along with the rest. After overextending himself in the fall of 1887, he decided, without his father's knowledge, to sell family property at the corner of Lake and Walnut streets in the Olivewood Tract. When the parcel was first acquired, Nathan had agreed with the tract's developer, C.T. Hopkins of San Francisco, to trade Elsinore lands for Olivewood. For reasons he did not reveal, Hopkins stipulated that Nathan not resell the Olivewood parcel to a Pasadena man by the name of John McCoy. Nathan consented, but before ownership of the property was finalized, he unaccountably accepted $1,000 from McCoy as deposit for the property.

Hopkins was irate. Nathan had gone completely against his word! John Yocum, having been told of his son's actions and thinking he would get him out of the scrape, immediately stepped in and purchased the Olivewood property for $16,000 from Hopkins.[3] Now McCoy became indignant; he still wanted the property, and Nathan had not even returned his deposit! McCoy started legal action for breach of contract against the Yocums, but the matter was quickly settled out of court with McCoy taking title to the Olivewood parcel for the original $10,000 price established by Nathan.[4]

On September 13, 1887, Nathan, then 28, went into Los Angeles on business related to the Hopkins deal. Late in the day he telegraphed his family that he had missed the last train home and would spend the night in the city. When he did not return the next day or the next, Yocum expressed fear that his son had been murdered.

Pasadena's Monk Hill, with Washington School, c. 1890. John Yocum lived on Monk Hill in 1883, and his view of Indian Flat (Linda Vista, left background) encouraged him to move there. La Cañada Valley is in the center background. *Courtesy Pasadena Historical Society.*

Newspapers carried the story on front pages. The Los Angeles *Times* described Nathan as "one of the most successful businessmen in Southern California" and reported that "the best detectives in the State have been working on the case."[5] Yocum announced in the *Daily News* that he would give a $2,500 reward for information concerning Nathan, dead or alive. The offer was soon withdrawn, however, when the family said they had at last heard from him.[6] They said he was in a confused state, and he would not reveal his place of self-imposed exile. Rumors circulated he had fled to the Fresno area. Finally, in late February of 1888, Hannah Yocum was quoted in the papers as saying her son had regained his health and would soon be home, but he never returned to Linda Vista.

In Park Place the well of buyers dried up. Those who had already purchased property abandoned their mortgages, and the developers put the houses up for rent. In an effort to bolster the dying tract, the *Daily Union* stated, "There has perhaps been no greater success in the financial history of Pasadena than that achieved by this firm" [Nathan's syndicate].[7]

According to the *Daily News,* the Park Place owners, having one year earlier each invested less than $1,000 in the project, took out profits of $25,000 before now closing the development.[8] Despite efforts to save Park Place, Nathan's syndicate dissolved in January 1888.

Even though the railway also failed to make money, daily trips to the Linda Vista community continued until 1892 when the service was shut down and the tracks sold to the Mount Lowe Railway.

Meanwhile, John Yocum's problems compounded. Both he and Nathan, along with the other syndicate members, were

Linda Vista, c. 1900, looking north to Yocum's ranch. Flintridge and La Cañada are over the ridge. *Courtesy Alice Wallace, Pasadena Historical Society, Linda Vista History Collection.*

accused of a great land-booming scheme at Lucerne. Legal suits were filed against all of the men. Yocum was charged with diverting area waters from canyons and sending it to syndicate property instead of letting it flow to land it should rightfully irrigate. Buyers had been misled, the accusation continued. Despite the diverted waters, the area turned out to be more water-poor wasteland than verdant paradise. Area coal mining rights, which the syndicate claimed as its own, were actually owned by another company.

Yocum responded:

> I am sorry...for all who suffer because of the collapse of everything at Lucerne. We go down with $100,000, Mr. H. with $20,000, as he reckons; a number of others with as much or more in proportion to their means; and who could have avoided the collapse? Who can indemnify?[9]

Charles A. Sawtelle served as the Yocum's attorney. Mundell, one of the syndicate members, took over the task of trying to settle Nathan's debts at Lucerne, as well as those of the Park Place Tract; Flynn and Ogden, the other two members, had since moved out of the area. In January 1888, attempting to untangle himself from a morass of increasing financial difficulties, John Yocum sold a large portion of his Linda Vista property for $68,000 to neighbor Byron Clark and to L.G. Kellogg.[10]

Shortly thereafter, John Yocum's creditors, including Clark, filed a suit against him, and Yocum was forced to turn Elsinore rights over to the courts. He was then declared an "insolvent debtor," held liable for Nathan's debts, and prevented temporarily from selling any more of their lands. In 1893 Yocum filed for bankruptcy.[11]

John, Hannah and Lydia Yocum withdrew into the Linda Vista farming community, which had continued with relative calm during the bust and now showed them empathy. John became ill and was confined to his home for a period of time. When he was able to work again, he made his primary business peach growing and drying. Finally, the courts allowed him to pay off his and Nathan's debts by selling many of their remaining properties in Linda Vista and Pasadena, as well as some they owned in Iowa.

John and Hannah took over the support of Nathan's family, which remained at their own farm house. Lydia undoubtedly visited Nathan after his 1887 disappearance, since Maurice Yocum, their youngest child, was born in 1890. (Arthur was born about 1885 and Louise in 1888.) Lydia and the children eventually relocated to the San Francisco area.

John Yocum had a brother named Aaron D. Yocum, called A.D. for short. When John moved to Pasadena from Iowa, A.D. was living in Kentucky, but in the early 1890s A.D., an unsuccessful attorney, moved with his wife to Pasadena to be near John. Besides being a comfort to his brother, A.D. also wanted to better his own situation by joining a small law office in Pasadena. When this practice faltered, he moved from his three-acre Lincoln Avenue home to Linda Vista to help John with the fruit growing.

A letter written by A.D. in 1886 to Lincoln historian Ward H. Lamon gives insight into Jane Yocum, John and A.D.'s mother. A.D. was badly wounded while serving with the Union army during the Civil War. Joan, intent on visiting him in the war-zone hospital, traveled to Washington, D.C. for permission, which was denied. She persisted with her efforts until she finally saw Mary Todd Lincoln's personal maid. The maid summoned Mrs. Lincoln. Listening to the distraught mother, Mrs. Lincoln took pity on her and brought the President. Mr. Lincoln heard her story and wrote out an order that enabled Jane Yocum to visit A.D. in the restricted zone, where she nursed him back to health.[12]

Linda Vista provided no solutions for A.D. and once more he returned to Pasadena, where his wife died in 1901. One year later, at Mountain View Cemetery in Pasadena, he shot himself to death on her grave. A.D.'s suicide note to John, stuck to the top of the grave with a knife, stated that life had been one long ordeal. The note ended "Brother J.D., farewell! I feel deeply for you. I know you will say I am insane. I will not deny it. I fear an asylum." The suicide and note were reported on the front-page of the *Daily News*. In the same article, Yocum was described as

"Professor J. Yocum of Linda Vista...one of the brainiest and most esteemed men in the community."[13]

John Yocum, unlike A.D., was resilient. He and Hannah continued to host new families arriving in Linda Vista. During Yocum's later years, he returned to real estate transactions while also farming land and drying fruit.

According to Los Angeles County death records, Hannah Yocum, still a Linda Vista resident with her husband, died of bronchitis in 1913 at the age of 83.[14] She was buried at Mountain View Cemetery, but her body was later disinterred and reburied at an unspecified location. California state probate records show that John Yocum died on about May 4, 1917 in Stockton, California, also at the age of 83.[15] He was undoubtedly staying with his grandson, Maurice, who lived in nearby Bellota. Louise and Arthur, the other two grandchildren, resided in San Jose at the time.

The events of the Yocums' days in Linda Vista are essentially tragic ones. Even though successful in developing their chosen site for a home and community, John and Hannah's life there was one of personal loss and financial misfortune. Much of their story suggests the ebullience of the real estate boom and then the disappointment arising out of the bust.

Byron Clark had joined with John and Nathan during the boom in several business enterprises. One such move was to invest in a large section of the Park Place Tract. When that venture began to falter, he unsuccessfully attempted to save the development by doing last-minute landscaping. His financial stability, however, crumbled from losses in the tract as well as from his earlier efforts in the olive oil and fruit crystallization industries. Finally, in the late 1890s, Clark sold his Linda Vista home to B. Frank Ball and moved his family to Hawaii, where he became active in pineapple growing. Relocating a few years later to Palo Alto, Clark died there in 1916.

The men who developed Linda Vista's hillsides were both risk-takers and prophets. Between 1871 and 1887 Benjamin Dreyfus grazed sheep on the hills, Moses Langley Wicks platted

Linda Vista oldtimers focussed on agrarian businesses. Here Mr. Blake surveys his bee hives. *Courtesy Dorn Family, Pasadena Historical Society, Linda Vista History Collection.*

the land, John D. Yocum developed it for farmland home sites, and Byron Clark beautified it with new plantings. These four men established a backdrop of crop raising, steady growth and community enterprise, and the real estate fall of the late 1880s had no lasting effect on the future they foresaw for the slopes.

Life Goes On

The present good conditions of development in Linda Vista have been preserved largely through the help of Pasadena people, for which, having already been personally profited, I wish to express my personal thanks. The part of Linda Vista not burned over last year, would without doubt have burned over this year if it had not been for the two hundred volunteers rushed to the scene through the efforts of Pasadena people. Keep an eye on us. We are worth it and will be an ornament to you yet!

> Mrs. R.M. Schoonmaker
> Letter to the Pasadena
> *Daily News,* September 2, 1910.

As Linda Vistans rallied around Hannah and John Yocum, their community displayed an innocence as well as a sense of cohesiveness. At the same time, newcomers continued to move there, attracted by the natural beauty of the slopes and the area's detachment from the swifter pace of Pasadena, now a hub of resort hotels and tourists.

Richard Dorn, a Canadian, was one of the first to arrive, living with the Yocums until he could build a five-room house north of Park Avenue, near Lida Street, and send for his family to join him. The family later moved to Linda Vista's Ontario Avenue.

The staying power of the Dorns is well illustrated by Richard's son, Arthur. Arthur was born at the Ontario Avenue home, lived on this block all his life, owned and operated a Pasadena auto repair shop for 55 years, and was married to the same woman for 65 years.

Blanche Dorn, Arthur's wife, wrote a vast manuscript about her life in Linda Vista, filling the pages with warm anecdotes.

Dorn family farmhouse, 1299 Linda Vista Avenue, built in 1887.
*Photo by Paul Cuen, Pasadena Historical Society, Linda Vista History
Collection.*

Her parents, the Mossholders, came to the Linda Vista community around 1902, buying their property from Yocum. Blanche
and Arthur attended school together, and after their marriage,
lived in the old schoolhouse, which had been moved to Ontario
Avenue and turned into a residence.

Typical of Blanche Dorn's bucolic narrative is her account of
Claudio, legendary character of Linda Vista. An Indian ward of a
La Canada doctor, Claudio endeared himself to the neighborhood
with his eccentricities, especially as a trader. One day he purchased with silver a derby hat from a local citizen. Thereafter,
he constantly wore the hat along with a red calico rag tied
beneath his chin as he wandered the Linda Vista streets.

United States census records for 1890 were lost in a fire, but
the 1900 census provides a partial list of Linda Vista residents,
from which the Yocums and others are unaccountably missing.[1]

Looking west across the arroyo to roads leading to Pasadena's Annandale section, c. 1905.

Looking west across what is now Brookside Park to Jumbo Knob and lower Linda Vista, c. 1905.

In the background, Linda Vista slopes led down to small farms located in what is now Brookside Park, c. 1905.

This 1905 photograph shows the upper end of Linda Vista, where orchards once flourished. The present-day Brookside Park area is in the foreground.

Linda Vista—1900 Census Report
(Number of family members)

Family	Origin	Trade
Dorn, Richard (5)	Canada	carpenter
Berriz (8)	Mexico	
Schibler, Hiram (6)	Germany	farmer
Dorn, Joseph (4)	Canada	carpenter
Lemocher, G. (6)	Switzerland	farmer
Reidebach, Henry (12)	Iowa	salesman
Woodruff, Charles	Illinois	
Helky, C. T. (8)	Virginia	farmer
Lloyd, P.W. (6)	England	carriage painter

In a small 1903 article, the Pasadena *Evening Star* reported fourteen dwellings in the "hamlet." Residents were listed as Wickham (owner of poultry, pigeons and a "thoroughbred jersey cow"), Williams (on a homestead formerly owned by the Dix family), Berraros (John Yocum's foreman), George Pierson, John Carson (one-time owner of the Linda Vista Hotel), Mrs. Griggs (another proprietor of the hotel), Corey, Costa and Hudson. More families continued to arrive, many leaving their mark on the community in one way or other.

The Prosser family came to Linda Vista in the early 1900s, living in the Yocums' original ranch house until they bought approximately twenty acres of property from Yocum near La Vista Place. On their land they graded dirt roads and erected small plank bridges. They also leveled a hilltop on which they put their home.

Reverend R.M. Schoonmaker, outgoing and civic-minded, moved with his family to Linda Vista in 1906. In 1914 Schoonmaker was elected president of the Linda Vista Improvement Association. (The word "Land" had by now been dropped from the organization's name.) A retired Methodist minister, Schoonmaker preached periodically at Pasadena churches. During the Depression of the 1930s, he could be seen driving his car with a sign on it advertising "Carpenter Work Done for Those Unable to Pay."[2]

In 1909 a fire swept through parts of Linda Vista, destroying two homes, heavily damaging the Linda Vista Bridge and killing two fire fighters. A new $20,000 concrete bridge was built to replace Yocum's earlier structure, and a thirteen-ton roller was dragged across the new bridge to test its strength.

The George Hoffman family moved to Linda Vista in 1911 from Illinois, and theirs is perhaps the most memorable family name of the community. Besides George, its members included his wife, Eleanore, and their children James, Halleck, Paul, Virginia and Marjorie. The family story integrates rural life with cosmopolitan activity.

George Hoffman invented the Hoffman valve before he moved to California. With the profits from this work, he purchased an old Linda Vista chicken ranch on seven acres of land formerly belonging to the Gallagher family. Further purchases expanded the family holding to 125 acres adjacent to the extensive holdings of W.R. Timkin.

Once in Linda Vista and using his home as a laboratory, George invented the Thermador heater. He also served as president of the American Radiator Company, operated out of an old barn, and took an active part in the experimental raising and propagating of the ranch's 1,800 avocado trees. Always trying to improve techniques, he had all family garbage buried in the orchards as fertilizer. In 1926 Hoffman, by now a millionaire, built a large English Tudor home at 1500 El Mirador Drive on a hilltop overlooking the slopes.

At the beginning of the Great Depression, and with the bank threatening to foreclose on his property, George sold many holdings, including a 71-foot yacht. He did manage to hang on to the Thermador Company. After his death in 1932, Eleanore continued to maintain the ranch with the help of her children. Veta Affleck, the local school teacher and principal, joined in the household to help. For years family members struggled to keep the ranch in the Hoffman name. Eleanore put in El Mirador Drive and sold 500-foot lots to pay the mortgage and water bills. She died in 1948, the same year that the Linda Ridge area was developed.

From the Hoffman's earliest days in Linda Vista, James Hoff-

The Hoffman homestead and El Mirador Dairy, 1920. Avocado orchards were another family enterprise. *Photo courtesy Charles Seims, Pasadena Historical Society, Linda Vista History Collection.*

The Hoffman residence under construction, c. 1922. *Photo courtesy Hoffman Family, Pasadena Historical Society, Linda Vista History Collection.*

man, a founder of Calavo (the California Avocado Growers' Association), managed the family ranch. From 1914 to 1929 he also developed and operated on the property the El Mirador Dairy. Approximately twelve employees ran the dairy, and several of them were provided with separate cottages in which to live. Dairy products were delivered to Pasadena, sometimes by one of the Hoffman sisters, but the award-winning dairy was more quaint then lucrative. Local competition came mainly between 1918 to 1922 from T.S. Kealey's dairy at 1636 Linda Vista Avenue. James Hoffman died at the ranch in 1950.

Halleck Hoffman, an inventor following in his father's footsteps, started on ranch premises the Halleck E. Hoffman Standard Record Manufacturing Company. He converted the barn into a tape recording studio where record masters were made on aluminum discs covered with lacquer. Seven employees worked full-time, and the factory lasted until 1945. Halleck died in 1951.

Paul G. Hoffman became the best known of George and Eleanore's children. In 1910 he began working as a janitor with the Studebaker Corporation in Chicago. When he moved to Pasadena with his family, he continued as a Los Angeles company salesman and won a national Studebaker sales contest in 1914. He was promoted to branch manager in 1917 and two years later he owned the Los Angeles retail branch. In 1935 Paul was named president of the Studebaker Corporation, a position he held until 1948.

Paul Hoffman is best remembered for his 1948-1950 administration of the Marshall Plan. As a progressive Republican, he incited the anger of McCarthy conservatives because of his positions in defense of trade unions, foreign aid and civil liberties. On the other hand, he earned the respect of many party members and was a personal friend and advisor of President Dwight D. Eisenhower. Hoffman was a United Nations delegate from 1956 to 1957, a top-ranking official of the United States Secretariat from 1959 to 1971, and a director of the Ford Foundation. He wrote three books: *Seven Roads to Safety, Peace Can Be Won,* and *World Without War.*

Throughout his life Hoffman, an inveterate family man, assisted financially in keeping the Linda Vista ranch in the family name. His wife, Dorothy Brown, and varying numbers of the couple's seven children, moved to the family home in 1945 while Hoffman traveled about on government jobs. Approximately six Studebakers of various colors and styles were parked around the ranch during these years, and whenever Hoffman returned to Linda Vista, his arrival caused excitement. Neighbors eagerly watched to see which cars were included in his entourage. On one occasion he brought a large trailer that could sleep eight and left it on the ranch grounds as a clubhouse for neighborhood children. Hoffman died in 1974.

Simultaneous with the Hoffman family, their avocado trees, inventions and dairy, a new breed of homeowner moved to Linda Vista—the Midwestern and Eastern entrepreneur, who "wintered" in southern California and kept an eye out for ways to invest his money, often in real estate.

Looking across from the present site of the Rose Bowl to the San
Gabriel Mountains, c. 1905.

CHAPTER FIVE

Transition

Why buy or build in an ugly place when scenic beauty may be had at no greater cost?. . . We took this into consideration in selecting the site for the houses we are building on Linda Vista Boulevard. . .[a] better location could scarcely have been found.

"The Bungalow Group"
an advertisement by the
Angeles Mesa Land Company, 1920.

The citizens of early Pasadena thought of their neighbors across the Arroyo as quaint, uncomplicated, folk, and this attitude was reflected in the local newspaper. An article on page one of the April 27, 1906 Pasadena *Daily Union* found great sport in reporting a victim of mistaken identity being chased through Linda Vista streets by a gun-wielding attacker. The paper's headline chortled, "Lively Mix Up in Linda Vista." Later, a 1907 edition of the paper chronicled a group of Linda Vista male residents, "hooligans," rattling windows of the local schoolhouse to show disapproval of a meeting held to discuss a proposed La Canada elevated railway. Such rib-poking on the part of the city aristocrats did not last, however, as Linda Vista soon became a favored location for the homes and real estate developments of wealthy Easterners and Midwesterners.

By the turn of the century, visitors had been arriving in Pasadena for many years, drawn by its healthful climate and its reputation as a center of wealth, culture and grace, albeit of the "Western" variety. If you belonged to the Eastern, monied establishment and had a yen to experience the frontier, this was the place to go, where edges were less rough and transitions less shocking than in most other Western enclaves.

A Brahmin might winter at one of Pasadena's famed hotels in comfort. Before dinner he could relax on the veranda, sip a glass of California wine, and study the late afternoon shadows on the mountain peaks. For intellectual stimulation there was entertainment at Pasadena's own opera house. If our traveler were of a more rugged bent, he could take the Mount Lowe Incline Railway 5,000 feet into the San Gabriel Mountains—or hike up and down the Arroyo. And if he got bored, true civilization, after all, cost only the price of a one-way Pullman ticket.

A handful of these visitors, experienced in the ways of business and with money to spend, joined the ranks of Linda Vistans. They discovered the allure of the slopes and were charmed by the winding roads and panoramic views. The land seemed valuable, not only as sites for wonderful homes for gracious living, but also for its proximity to Pasadena. With entrepreneurial abandon these millionaires gave form to their ideas and triggered Linda Vista's gradual transition from rustic farming community to affluent residential area.

Ohio's William Robert Timken, vice president and treasurer of Timken Roller Bearing Company, was one such person who spent winters in Pasadena. In the early 1900s he bought substantially all of Linda Vista north of El Mirador. Not only did he put up chalets to lodge his numerous guests, but paths snaked over his land, connecting the family house with the cottages.

A major Timken project was a road cutting across the property and up the hills to a retreat house at the crest. Clarence Day, nationally renowned engineer, was the road's contractor. In 1919 *California Southland* magazine reported:

> Up on the highest ridge of Linda Vista there has been built a private road that by its very grade insures seclusion. Like Napoleon when he demanded for his troops a straight road to Moscow, the owner of a mountain bungalow has drawn a line straight up the hogback of the hills; and engineers with modern skill have built the road it indicates.[1]

Timken also joined promoter Freeman Ford (the 1901 founder of the Pasadena Ice Company) and attorney Judson R. Rush in

Clarence Day, c. 1930, Timken's road construction engineer. *Courtesy Pasadena Historical Society.*

developing a 1920s tract known as Rancho Linda Vista, part of Dr. Hodge's former property.

C.B. Van Every and Jack Teegarden bought large amounts of Linda Vista acreage during the early 1900s. Van Every's name appears on countless early land records. Teegarden purchased the McCormick farm that spread north from the Linda Vista Bridge (also known as the Holly Street Bridge), and Teegarden supervised 1907 work on a road that led up through his property and over the ridge into the Annandale area.

M. Cochrane Armour, president from 1900 to 1917 of the Iroquois Iron Company of Chicago, was the first millionaire to launch the era of imaginative homes in Linda Vista. Escaping from the cold of Illinois in 1905, Armour, then in his 50s, enjoyed numerous winters in southern California, finally deciding to move west for good. Always one with a sense of business and enough cash reserves and financial acumen to guarantee success, he began developing tracts. His connection with the community stretched over a twenty-year period.

In a 1909 $100,000 cash deal, Armour purchased 65 acres of the Webster property. This land, which Armour lined with acacia trees, extended westward from the Arroyo to the top of the ridge and northward from the Linda Vista Bridge, including Mira Vista Terrace. He subdivided 22 acres of the land into the Arroyo View Tract, and 200-foot frontage lots with $5,000 minimum building restrictions guaranteed substantial homes.[2] Neighbors to the north listened, fascinated, to rumors that Armour intended to turn the area into a park rivaling Pasadena's Busch Gardens.

J. Constantine Hillman, Armour's personal friend and architect for the very rich, designed many of the homes in Armour's tract. In 1911 he fashioned an $8,000, two-story chalet at 405 Mira Vista Terrace for George Howard Crosby. Hillman built another chalet at 343 Mira Vista Terrace near Crosby's for Mary J. Hamlin.

Crosby was a wealthy industrialist from Minnesota, who spent the five coldest months of each year at Linda Vista.[3] He

Looking west across the Arroyo to Linda Vista with the La Cañada Valley to the right, c. 1910.

The Scoville bridge, dam and pump house, early 1900s, prominent features of the arroyo just south of the Armour property. *Courtesy Pasadena Historical Society.*

served as president of Crosby Motor Company, Crosby Exploration Company, and Crosby Water, Light and Power Company, all in the Duluth area. He was also owner of numerous mines and brick manufacturing plants and was a national director of the American Red Cross.

The Crosby house received disapproval because of the large windows that went across the front of the house. Critics said the windows would make the structure too warm in the summertime. But this hardly concerned Crosby as he was never there at that time anyway. He was more interested in winter views of the San Gabriels.

In 1912 Hillman designed and built Armour a house at 280 Linda Vista Avenue near the Scoville property. The contractor was Peter Hall, a close associate of leading Pasadena architects Charles and Henry Greene. J. Salter created a Craftsman gateway for the place. The house (extensively remodeled) and gate still stand, remnants of the Arts and Crafts movement of the day.

The architect for Armour's ultimate residence was David Ogilvie. He designed an eighteen-room villa for 950 Holly Vista

Drive, high on a hill above Jumbo Knob. Built in 1925 the home
and grounds cost $90,000, a large amount of money at that time.[4]
The estate's drive, with a 1,200-foot-long, rose-covered fence,
reflected Armour's keen interest in landscaping. Several acres of
fruit trees, an artificial lake and two lily ponds accentuated the
home's Mediterranean design. Armour died in 1928.

Another wealthy investor sinking money into Linda Vista
developments was William S. Mason of Chicago, who wintered
for over thirty years at his 100 Los Altos Drive home. In 1913 he
formed the San Rafael Improvement Company with several other
wealthy Chicago speculators. In 1923 these men purchased 65
acres for a tract development running from the Arroyo boundary
of the Scoville estate north to the Armour property, land owned
by Charles B. Scoville for the previous 25 years. Prominent
architect Myron Hunt laid out the tract, and homes appeared
along twisting hillside roads.

In 1913 in a reciprocal arrangement with the city of Pasadena,
Armour and neighbor Mason allowed the city a right-of-way
through their property for a road to new Brookside Park, land necessary for convenient access to the recreational facility. In return
the city had large Arroyo boulders hauled up from the stream bed
and used to construct walls alongside roads on Armour's and
Mason's properties.

Mason was a member of the board of trustees of Pomona
College and in 1915 gave this institution his collection of Western
Americana, the nucleus for the special collection of Pomona
College's Honnold Library. The collection originally held 233
books and thirteen maps dealing mainly with the early exploration and settlement of the West Coast, and Mason continued
adding to the count. He also gave Yale University, his alma mater,
a holding of Benjamin Franklin materials and donated funds to
Yale for the Mason Laboratory of Engineering.

Bela Otis Kendall was not a rich man when he arrived with
his wife in Pasadena from Massachusetts. However, by saving
the money he earned working as a vacuum cleaner salesman, he
was able to open a four-room real estate office at the site of the

present Pasadena YMCA. Kendall eventually became one of the city's top real estate developers, amassing a fortune by dealing in Pasadena area properties, including Linda Vista. He put up numerous buildings (the Central Building, the Boston Building and the Kinney-Kendall Building) and figured prominently in construction on Raymond Avenue and Colorado Street. He also made an 1895 map of Pasadena, which excludes the Linda Vista area, a touchstone to the times. From 1926 to 1936 his residence was a Bennett and Haskell home at 500 Linda Vista Avenue.

Kendall did not restrict himself to real estate; he was affiliated with the National Bank of Pasadena and was president of the Pasadena Theater Company, the Tournament of Roses and the Crown Transfer and Storage Company. In 1938 he retired to Catalina Island, where he had maintained a summer residence for years and where he died in 1942.

Linda Vista was already attracting attention when a Pasadena *Star* writer commented in 1911:

What I hope to see some day is an eight or ten-mile auto-

These early Linda Vista Avenue grounds and modest structures were soon replaced by the B.O. Kendall estate. *Courtesy Hofgaarden Family, Pasadena Historical Society, Linda Vista History Collection.*

mobile and carriage road along the slopes and over the summit on the hills on the west side of the Arroyo Seco opposite Pasadena. That territory should by right be a part of Pasadena.... The view from the top of these hills is magnificent, especially in the late afternoon when the sun is sinking in the west and the whole city is sketched against the mountains, themselves aglow with purple light. Nor should this matter be postponed too long. The first thing we know the summits of these hills will be cut into villa lots and some of our opportunities gone.[5]

Wealthy investors continued to settle in Linda Vista and develop tracts. W.F. Normandy (Normandy Lane) of Salt Lake City was joined by Francis J. Walker, vice-president of Blankenhorn Realty, and the two bought and subdivided 35 acre-parcels of J.M. Jensen's widespread holding in south Linda Vista.

Horace M. Dobbins, Pasadena mayor from 1900 to 1902, had an extravagant idea for the hills behind Linda Vista. Dobbins, who had built Pasadena's elevated wooden cycleway—a curious structure that extended in the early 1900s for two miles between the Green Hotel and Glenarm Street—bought up all of Jumbo Knob, portions at a time. He held the land until he could figure out the perfect plan for its use.

Finally, in 1924 Dobbins announced that he would create a winding road leading to the summit of Jumbo Hill ("Knob" had now been replaced by the more sedate "Hill"), with trees and vines planted on either side. The development was to be called Rodela del Sol (Target of the Sun), and architect Wallace Neff would be responsible for the layout of the road and home sites. At the time, Neff was inspired by the romanticism of popular films, and his idea was for the hillsides to have the overall appearance of a Spanish hill town, somewhat like old Toledo. The skyline drive would eventually stretch the entire length of the hill tops between San Rafael and Flintridge, dotting the area with Mediterranean villas. The project offended traditionalists, however, and only the Jumbo Hill part of Dobbins' dream materialized.

Edward M. Fowler combined creative and practical talents in his Linda Vista real estate transactions. The son of Edward

Payson Fowler, a noted pioneer in bacteriology, Edward M. moved to Pasadena around 1909. A graduate of Yale University and New York University Law School, Fowler pursued a number of careers: freelance writer, foreign correspondent, cotton goods manufacturer and exporter, architect and real estate investor. In the latter endeavor he joined with Robert M. Modisette to found Pasadena's Fowler-Modisette Realty Company.

Fowler was known as an architectural copyist, specializing in Majorcan and Andalusian designs. In 1928, one year before he died, he built a home for himself at 825 Las Palmas Road. The Andalusian house remains today, with the 134 Freeway span looming dramatically overhead.

The president of both the First Trust and Savings Bank and the First National Bank of Pasadena, Robert Modisette specialized in building, financing and development. He produced with Fowler a number of Pasadena and Linda Vista homes. Modisette, originally from Minneapolis, lived at 405 Linda Vista Avenue.

Not all 1920s real estate ventures in Linda Vista were for the rich. In 1924 the Angeles Mesa Company developed small, moderately priced homes in the vicinity of Lida Street and Linda Vista Avenue. These homes ranged from $6,000 to $9,500 and advertisements proclaimed their stucco construction, hardwood floors, and gas floor heaters.[6]

In 1926 contractor John B. Hall laid the foundations for nine cottages as part of a Linda Vista bungalow court to be built on one lot. Concerned residents immediately acted, and the city enforced the provision of a zoning act ruling out such crowded construction. The foundations were removed.

Other illustrious Linda Vista residents of the early 1900s were Judge Kenneth Newell; James Williams, president of the Pasadena Chamber of Commerce; William R. Staats; Harry Chandler; J.P. Clifford, president of Cream of Wheat; and F.P. Chesebrough.

Hotel magnate Daniel M. Linnard lived at 809 Linda Vista Avenue also during the 1920s. At one time or another he was associated with the Maryland, Vista del Arroyo, Huntington and

Green hotels in Pasadena and the Fairmont Hotel in San Francisco. He also ran large hotels in Los Angeles, New York City and Atlantic City. As president of the Pasadena Board of Trade, he once said that there would always be a Rose Parade even if his were the only entry and he had to push a wheelbarrow down Colorado Boulevard!

An anomaly occurred when Mr. and Mrs. Hiram W. Wadsworth built a two-story log cabin at 1145 Linda Vista Avenue. The cabin was used as a retreat by the Wadsworths before they relocated there in 1933. This craftsman house was a sharp contrast to the sprawling Mediterranean-style homes of people such as Linnard, Armour and Modisette. The structure still stands, a testimony to the wide range of architectural designs in the community.

Wadsworth's business was in painting supplies, but he absorbed himself in other activities as well, serving for six years on Pasadena's Board of Directors. He was also on the Board of Directors of California Institute of Technology and president of the Colorado River Aqueduct Association from 1924 to 1929. Shortly before his 1939 death, a Pasadena *Star News* article proclaimed, "The Metropolitan Water District Aqueduct and Pasadena Civic Center are, in a sense, monuments to Mr. Wadsworth."[7]

Finally, the history of the Pegfair estate sums up the changes that have occurred in Linda Vista over the years, with land ownership moving from farmer to entrepreneur and tract developer. The Pegfair story dates back to 1887 when the Chamberlain family bought 220 acres of Yocum property, land situated around Wellington Ave. and north towards Lida Street. The Chamberlains built a farm house and barn on the hill where Pegfair now stands, and they planted the surrounding property with peach trees. In 1907 Marshall D. Fiscus bought the property and named the house Hillcrest.

Robert J. Richards, a produce executive, and his wife, Arabella, purchased the property in 1929 and built a $40,000, fourteen-room, 9,000-square-foot mansion at 1211 Wellington Ave. They named their mansion Fairview. John Pederson designed the home,

An aerial view of the modern-day Pegfair estate. *Courtesy Pasadena Historical Society, Linda Vista History Collection.*

working closely with local architect Garrett Van Pelt. Tiles by famed Craftsman tilemaker Ernest A. Batchelder decorate the kitchen and library, and some rooms have marble fireplaces. Fairview was put up for auction in 1939, and Wesley I. Dumm bought the property for $200,000. He renamed the place Pegfair after his second wife, Margaret.

Dumm, the son of a Methodist minister, was born in Ohio in 1890. He financed his own education at Ohio Wesleyan University before moving in 1924 to San Francisco where he busied himself with the banking business and with broadcasting. During World War II he was selected by President Franklin Roosevelt to build and operate an international short wave station for broadcasting to servicemen. Dumm later founded the Muzart Company, a Muzak franchise.

To assure his family's privacy, in 1954 Dumm acquired fourteen lots behind Pegfair. He later sold some of them for the Pegfair Estates Tract. Additional lots were sold in 1960 to the Art

Center College of Design, with the stipulation that the property be preserved in its natural setting. Part of the less hilly portion north and south of Lida Street was sold for subdivision.

The Dumm family lived in Linda Vista for 20 years. During this time Dumm became involved in southern California philanthropies, helping to found the Pasadena Museum of Art and the Los Angeles Zoo and participating in the affairs of the Claremont School of Theology. Finally, in 1969, selling Pegfair and its adjacent property to Mr. and Mrs. Howard Arndt, Dumm moved to La Jolla, where he died in 1977 at the age of 87.

In 1976 Pegfair was the Pasadena Junior Philharmonic's Showcase House of Interior Design. In 1978 George Gradow, a 35-year-old bachelor millionaire, bought the estate. Gradow threw lavish parties. At an "old fashioned Labor Day picnic," guests were required to dress entirely in white. The tradition of Linda Vista's colorful millionaires dies slowly.

Wealthy investors and homeowners changed forever the tone of Linda Vista. By the 1920s concerns developed over uncontrolled growth. Although the hillsides were still "secluded and picturesque," this ambience was threatened by the continued arrival of new residents and ambitious land speculators.

CHAPTER SIX

Sustaining the Garden Paradise

> Beware the isolated life and the smug satisfaction
> which often goes with it. You owe much to the
> community in which you live. Leaven the lump.
> Not one of you liveth to himself.
>
> > John Willis Baer
> > 809 Linda Vista Avenue
> > President of Occidental
> > College, 1906-1916

Commercial and public-oriented ventures were launched through the early years in Linda Vista, fostered by the residents. The Park Nursery, a private business, had been the first such enterprise. Word of Byron Clark's horticultural skills spread throughout the San Gabriel Valley and curious visitors found their way to the slopes. After the nursery, a public school was the next organized project.

Linda Vista School, which celebrated its centennial in 1988, grew from a one-room frame building with eleven students to its present facility with approximately 375 students.[1] The Land and Improvement Association enlisted Richard Dorn and James Agar to erect the $700 school building on Yocum property, and the school opened in November 1888 as Andrew Jackson School, a part of the Pasadena School District.[2] Lydia Burson served as the first teacher-principal. A pot-bellied stove warmed the schoolhouse while an outhouse graced the backyard. When school hours were over, the building was a handy place for the few farming community families to hold meetings and social events.

By 1891 student ranks had grown from eleven to eighteen students, and Ella G. Wood was in charge. That same year Pasadena residents voted down a special $6,000 school tax.[3] The school board refused to pay for a teacher at Andrew Jackson, and the school closed and Linda Vista children were required to travel to Pasadena to attend Washington School.

When new funds became available, the school building was moved to Bryant Street and Wellington Avenue, where it reopened in 1903 as Linda Vista School. Isabel McAdam, the new teacher-principal, drove to work in a pony cart from her home on the east bank of the Arroyo, picking up stray children who wanted rides. McAdam taught eight grades with a total of thirty-four students, and she started the popular tradition of a family Christmas party, complete with popcorn strings and lighted candles decorating a ceiling-tall tree.

As student numbers increased, members of the Linda Vista Land and Water Company, a new epithet for the Land and Improvement Association, voted to build a larger school. The original building was moved in 1911 to 1340 Ontario Avenue, where it became a residence, and a new school was erected and named William Cullen Bryant School. By 1920, to alleviate crowded conditions, a one-room bungalow was moved onto the property. Next came the addition of a school auditorium.

In 1927, against some neighborhood protest, a second floor was added to the school, and the facility reverted back to its old name of the Linda Vista School. The second floor served first as an attic and then as four classrooms, but there were problems. A fire burned a portion of the second floor, and one night an upstairs pipe burst. A teacher arrived in the morning to find water seeping out from under the front door. The main two-story building was torn down in 1969 because it did not conform to earthquake safety standards, and a new one was erected.

One name stands out in connection with the school, teacher-principal Veta Affleck. Affleck was highly respected in the community and a crowd gathered in the early 1940s for a testimonial reception at the Huntington Hotel upon her retirement after thirty-three years with the school.

Affleck's story begins in 1920 when she first visited Pasadena. She did not intend to stay, but the district school superintendent asked, "Would you mind teaching in a school a little way out?" She later remarked,

> Linda Vista was a long way out . . . and the one school building was—well, a little below my expectations for all the schools I had seen in Pasadena were large, modern buildings. A view of that little old country schoolhouse almost scared me out. I had taught in a city before and was I now to come down to teaching in a "little, old red school house"?[4]

Affleck, who never married, had other interests besides teaching; she painted, drew, wrote poetry, sang with a perfectly pitched voice, and designed and made "Veta" dolls, dollhouses and furniture, which she sold through Straus and Company in New York City. After her retirement, she moved to Rancho Bernardo to be near relatives and where she bought her first house. She has since died.

Linda Vista School was once the home of a community Sunday school. Basically religious people, the early Linda Vistans felt handicapped by travel distances to and from church in Pasadena. Roads were bad during rainy weather, and crossing the Arroyo could be tricky. Residents solved the problem by starting a religious program for their children in the schoolhouse. The first session was held in 1903, and classes continued for a number of years, staffed by students' parents.

In 1907 a group of mothers met to hear a talk by Mrs. Lon F. Chapin, president of the Pasadena Garfield Child Study Circle. Enthusiastic about Chapin's ideas on child raising, the women decided to form their own study group and elected Mrs. C.E. Mills as president, Edith Mossholder as vice-president, and Mrs. Ralph Prosser as secretary. Within a few years, Mrs. Marshall Fiscus was organizing Red Cross work at the school, and by 1917 it became expedient to combine forces—the study group and the Red Cross unit became the Linda Vista PTA with Mrs. R. Ruhman as president.

Throughout the years, the PTA functioned as a way for young Linda Vista families to meet. It also performed its share of good works, organizing Red Cross Unity during World War II and purchasing war savings bonds and "blackout" curtains. Victory Gardens thrived.

Residents did not enthusiastically welcome the 1908 arrival of the Linda Vista health camp for low-income tuberculosis patients. The camp was the idea of S. Hazard Halstead, president of the Pasadena Ice Company and chairman of the Associated Charities of Pasadena.[5] Camp organizers procured a parcel of land on Linda Vista Avenue, with resident Caroline Wakeley adding an adjoining lot. A canvas-roofed cottage soon housed a number of patients. Future plans called for more tent cottages, but a local Linda Vista citizens' movement strongly objected, and with Reverend Ralph M. Schoonmaker presiding they threatened legal action. The camp directors, recognizing local hostility, relocated their project at the foothills above Altadena and named their camp La Vina Sanitarium. Area resident Charles Scoville assisted with financing the move.[6]

In the early twentieth century, water supplied by springs, tunnels, homemade canals and community pipes were insufficient for the population's needs. In 1910 the Pasadena *Daily News* published an irate letter from Mrs. Schoonmaker concerning the unfairness of the community's water assessments, the pirating of hillside reservoir waters, and preferential treatment for directors of the local water company. Something must be done, she wrote.[7]

By 1914 residents seeking Pasadena annexation completed a required petition, and the "trans-Arroyo" election was held August 17, 1914, and involved the Linda Vista, Annandale and San Rafael areas. The vote west of the Arroyo was 2,708 for annexation and 199 against. The city then voted in favor of the proposition by a fifteen to one majority, making the annexation the largest land procurement by Pasadena to that date.[8]

In celebration, newly annexed Linda Vista immediately and successfully made a formal request of the city to change the name of Park Avenue to Linda Vista Avenue. Street numbering was fixed by Pasadena city engineers and upon the petition of tract owner J.M. Jensen, who prepared to re-plat old Yocum property he had purchased, certain streets were entirely vacated. Pasadena water that had formerly been supplied to the community by water wagon was now piped through water main extensions paid for in part by the residents. The city also permitted bus service from Linda Vista into downtown Pasadena, with four trips a day at 9 and 11 and at 2 and 5.

One of Linda Vista's earliest businesses was the Linda Vista Hand Laundry, owned and operated by the William Dixon family from approximately 1915 to 1934. The green, wooden laundry building still stands behind the house at 800 Linda Vista Avenue.

In the early 1900s, before annexation, citizens paid for the oiling of Park Avenue, a dusty and rutted one-lane main street. A former front-porch stand that sold honey, eggs and garden vegetables was upgraded to a country market by a Mr. Vail and later moved across the street from where Jurgensen's market once stood. The business at 1987 Linda Vista Avenue changed hands several times; editions of the *City Directory* list various owners: G.F. Whitcomb (1914-1916), Annie Winchell (1917-1918), W.C. Codrick (1919) and Mrs. F.M. Bird (1919-1920).

The John Q. Tefft family purchased the store in 1920 and expanded it to include a small hand-pump gasoline station. Assorted livestock were kept in the back. Residents walked to the store and bartered homegrown fruits and vegetables for canned goods. Once, during an especially rainy year when Devil's Gate Dam overflowed, the Tefft daughters sold popcorn to sightseers passing through the neighborhood. On New Year's Day, with the Rose Parade nearby, the girls helped their mother sell hot dogs, drinks and candy to people walking to the event. Mr. Tefft sold spaces in the store parking lot.

When a 1909 fire damaged John Yocum's West Pasadena Railway bridge across the Arroyo, a reinforced concrete span, adequate for increased traffic, replaced it that same year. By 1922 this bridge was labeled dangerous and unsightly; age and disrepair had made questionable the weight it was capable of holding.

Finally, in 1924, as part of a training project by a California

Smoke rises from the Linda Vista bridge after a Caltech demolition crew's effort to destroy it. *Courtesy Wallace Family, Linda Vista History Collection, Pasadena Historical Society.*

Institute of Technology team of "demolition experts" (reserve engineers), the 1909 bridge was destroyed. Hundreds of spectators on the Arroyo banks watched in anticipation, waiting for the spectacle. To the embarrassment of the budding engineers, ten charges of TNT were fired without effect, and blasting was halted because of damage to windows and chandeliers in homes on nearby Linda Vista Avenue. A fence and shed at the 809 Linda Vista Avenue home of Daniel M. Linnard were damaged.

The blasting resumed and at last the bridge crashed to a rubble heap on the Arroyo bed. A new bridge was erected, made to be compatible with the nearby 1912-1913 Colorado Street bridge. The Seco Street bridge at Washington Boulevard was not built until 1939.

In 1921 a public road was completed approximating Timken's old road. Today this street, Lida Street, goes up the hills behind Linda Vista, past the Art Center College of Design, crosses over the ridge and then connects on the Glendale side with Figueroa Street and Chevy Chase Drive.

House numbers on the slopes were changed during the 1920s. The stretch of street from the Linda Vista Bridge to Orange Grove Boulevard was renamed Holly Street, and houses on Linda Vista Avenue and various side streets were renumbered, which explains the inconsistency in house numbers in early editions of the *City Directory.* The section of Linda Vista Avenue that runs between the Linda Vista Bridge and San Rafael Avenue was renamed Puente Avenue and then changed back to Linda Vista Avenue.

As more people arrived and more buildings appeared in Linda Vista, residents banded together in 1924 and formed the Linda Vista Neighborhood Association, the oldest neighborhood organization in Pasadena. (The association was an echo of the old Land and Improvement Association.) The group's name was changed to the Linda Vista-Annandale Association in the 1970s to include the residents south of the Linda Vista area. Today, homeowners in the area automatically become members and receive a quarterly newsletter; however, paid memberships are encouraged.

The association took action in 1924 to obtain street improvements under the guidelines of the Municipal Improvement Act of 1915. Petitions were circulated and signatures showed that close to 100 percent of the homeowners desired improvements. The city council issued appropriate bonds and work was begun. At a cost of approximately $800,000, streets were paved and sidewalks built, sewer laterals put in, utility lines installed undergound and ornamental lights placed along the streets. It was the "largest public improvement progam ever launched in Pasadena."[9]

A unique problem confronted the community in the late 1920s, resulting in a furor amongst the citizens of Linda Vista. Flintridge residents announced their intention to have the name of Linda Vista Avenue changed to Flintridge Boulevard. Republican United States Senator Frank P. Flint, Flintridge homeowner and southern California real estate developer, had built the Flintridge Biltmore Hotel on a southern hillside overlooking Linda Vista and Pasadena. The Flintridge townspeople argued to officials that the street leading to the hotel from Pasadena would be more appropriately named after the hotel, but the newly formed Linda Vista Association blocked the change.[10] The hotel complex is now occupied by the Flintridge Sacred Heart Academy.

That same year a local fire station was deemed necessary because of Linda Vista's usually dry hillsides. Designed by local architect William J. Stone to have the appearance of a Spanish residence, Engine House Number Eight opened its doors at 1150 Linda Vista Avenue on April 9, 1931. Four days later company fire fighters rushed to their first two fires. They doused flaming brush on Linda Vista Avenue and put out a garage fire on Las Lunas Street. In both instances the fires were extinguished before Central Station units arrived. In 1958 the station's structure was replaced with a ranch-style building.

In 1941 Harold Jurgensen bought the old Tefft market on Linda Vista Avenue from the Newmark family, and a popular tradition started in Linda Vista—Jurgensen's market. At this time several other businesses were attempting to establish themselves along Linda Vista Avenue, and the Linda Vista-Annandale Association raised approximately $2,000 to combat the commercialization of the area. Jurgensen was the only person able to obtain a city variance to operate a business on the slopes.

Jurgensen's prospered to such an extent that the market's original 3,000-square foot facility proved inadequate, and in 1957 it was enlarged to 5,500 square feet. The extension of the arcaded front was a prominent feature of designer Theodore Pletsch's ranch style building. Throughout the years the market and its country-like atmosphere endeared itself to the community, serving not only as a grocery store but also as a place to meet and chat with neighbors. For the 75th birthday celebration of the Linda Vista School, Jurgensen provided a cake approximately three-and-a-half-feet wide by one-foot long, sculpted in the school's shape.

By 1985, however, the eight-store Jurgensen chain was losing money, unable to compete with mammoth supermarkets. In 1986 it merged with the Yucaipa Capital Corporation, and the Linda Vista store was shut down the following year. In January 1988, the Jurgensen chain was sold to Ojai Capital, a partnership including longtime Pasadena residents. Since then the building has been razed and several homes are now on the property.

As the Linda Vista School grew, so did the desire of the students' mothers for more cohesiveness. The organization known as the Linda Vistans started as a small gathering of mothers picking up their children from school. The women waited at a nearby home, and as they grew in numbers, they decided to form a social group. "Know Your Neighbor" meetings were held in 1945 at various homes with all area women welcome. Soon the agenda included community concerns. In 1946 members chose the official name of Linda Vistans. Through the years, events have featured fund raisers for Pasadena-area charities and social events such as picnics at Pegfair, a bridge group, an annual strawberry festival and day-trips to nearby points of interest.

Talk of a Linda Vista branch of the Pasadena Public Library accompanied the building boom following World War II. The small library run at the school was no longer sufficient; by 1946 Linda Vista's population had grown to nearly 2,700. When in 1950 the Pasadena librarian recommended that every person living in the city should have access to a library within a mile's distance, 322 Linda Vista residents signed and presented a petition to the city to build an area branch. Another group of residents presented a petition asking that the site of the new branch be next to Jurgensen's and the fire station on Linda Vista Avenue, thereby creating a sort of neighborhood civic center. City officials preferred Wellington Avenue across from the school, feeling it could better service student needs at that location. This latter plan was adopted, and the 3,500-square foot, $56,000 library designed by Marion J. Varner opened on January 29, 1957.[11]

The Linda Vista Friends of the Library was formed in 1963. Over the years this group has purchased materials for the library such as furniture, books, magazines and newspapers and has arranged cultural programs.

In 1976 the city recommended closing the library, saying that the neighborhood was too small to warrant its own branch and suggesting the use of the facility as the school kindergarten. The idea met with strong resistance, and citizens successfully argued that the library provided many other services besides book lending—it sponsored a number of events ranging from PTA meetings to lectures and chamber music concerts. Still another attempt was made to close the library following the passage in 1978 of Proposition 13. This effort also failed.

Perhaps the most incongruous yet satisfactory new development in Linda Vista occurred in 1977—the establishment in the community of the Art Center College of Design, a behemoth compared to other area institutions. This 175-acre complex is completely modern, contrasting starkly to most of the other neighborhood structures, yet blending into the environment. The dramatic concrete and glass building sits on a hilltop overlooking the slopes, and far from being an eyesore, it serves as a reminder that the traditional and the modern can live comfortably side by side.

The Art Center was founded in 1930 by Edward A. Adams

The Art Center College of Design is built in the Miesian tradition and resembles a train racing across the landscape. *Photo by Steven A. Heller, Linda Vista History Collection, Pasadena Historical Society.*

and was first located in Los Angeles near MacArthur Park and then in the Hancock Park area. Under the leadership of its second president, Donald Kubly, the college moved to the top of Lida Street. The campus itself is situated on 15 acres and the total 175-acre property acts as a natural firebreak for the neighborhood properties.

When first announced, the proposed sale of the Dumm land for the Art Center received strong opposition from numerous area residents, particularly those living in the Pegfair Estates tract. These people were concerned that college students would create heavy traffic loads and noise and that the construction might eventually expand beyond the proposed site. However, the citizens of Linda Vista endorsed the project at a meeting held at the Pasadena Art Museum in April 1971. The Pasadena *Star News* reported in March 1973, "In obtaining a use permit for its 175-acre campus . . . the college pledged that for the first 20 years it would limit its use of the property to 30 acres, leaving the remainder in its natural state."[12]

Craig Ellwood and Associates designed the Art Center's bridge-like structure. The plans called for a 165,000 square-foot college costing $6,500,000. The overall cost with land, structure, equipment and site preparation eventually came to $8,500,000. John Dreyfuss of the Los Angeles *Times* called the building a "hill sculpture" that from a distance has "the grace and power of a train rushing across a high trestle."[13] Black steel diagonals are used for supports and duct work, and the sprinkler systems, electrical conduits, plumbing and massive steel beams are exposed and painted a flat black. The architectural design is "Miesian," in the manner of Mies van der Rohe, a pioneer of modern design geometry.

Since its inception, the college has grown in stature as an internationally influential school of design. The curriculum includes communication arts, industrial design and fine arts. Work has currently been done on automotive design and prototype space-station living quarters and galleys. Students design exhibits and a sculpture garden attracts visitors. The college is fully accredited and offers both bachelor's and master's degrees to its 1,150 students. Some 450 working professionals attend the Art Center at night.

Over the years the college's horizons have expanded. In October 1986, a European campus opened in a renovated century-old farm building at La Tour de Peilz, Switzerland. In 1987 the Art Center's first public drive was launched with its goal set at 25 million dollars. Recently, 47,000 square feet were added to the existing structure in Linda Vista.

Donald Kubly retired on December 31, 1985 after sixteen years as president of the college. David Brown, formerly communications vice president at Champion International, a paper company, took over Kubly's position.

Citizen groups, private industry, and city departments have worked together continuously on zoning and environmental regulations effecting Linda Vista. The Linda Vista-Annandale Association guards the hillsides from exploitation. In 1959 they oversaw a regulation limiting lot sizes to a minimum of 20,000 square feet. They also successfully supported a 1980 ordinance requiring the preservation of the rural atmosphere in new developments. A recent case illustrates the effectiveness of such ordinances—a Palos Verdes development company unsuccessfully attempted to win approval for thirty-eight duplex units on what was once the Hoffman property. Area sentiment has always been strongly against having anything except single-unit dwellings in Linda Vista.

Almost 100 acres of the old Hoffman ranch, Pasadena's largest undeveloped parcel, remained natural terrain until 1983, when, like Pegfair property, the ranch finally yielded to the subdividers. Developers Bill Rheinschild and Al Moreno graded roads and created homesites for the El Mirador Ranch tract. Years of negotiations went into restrictions placed upon the land's developers. An original request to build 100 homes was denied, and instead seventy percent of the land was set aside as permanent open space and the contractor held responsible for maintaining landscaping of vacant lots until all properties were sold. Project work was to be completed eighteen months after started. The El

The El Mirador Ranch development, 1987, on property that was once the Hoffman Ranch. *Photo by Garaint Smith, Linda Vista History Collection, Pasadena Historical Society.*

Mirador Ranch tract, with homes now priced at over one million dollars, received a 1987 award from the Pacific Coast Builders Conference in San Francisco for being the most outstanding residential site plan in the western United States.

The landscaping of Linda Vista streets and traffic islands received a boost when the Linda Vista-Annandale Association gathered money from citizen contributions and fund raisers to plant 306 trees. Strategically positioned boulders have also been placed on the dirt beyond some street curbs to discourage Rose Bowl parking.

Timken, Dumm, Armour and other early real estate developers did not face the restrictions later established in Linda Vista. Present-day homeowner's continued limits are necessary to ensure that the environment that attracted early residents changes as little as possible.

CHAPTER SEVEN

An Assemblage of Noted Residents

A painter is an asset to a community. He may not be a great commercial activity, but indirectly he acts enormously for the good of the place, just the way rhubarb is good for the system, or snail-eating ducks for the garden. He is as good advertising as you can get. . . . He doesn't cost the Chamber of Commerce a cent, but incidentally he is one of their biggest folders. . . . Vive l'Arroyo."

Medora Clark,
California Southland
(1923).

Early farmers gave Linda Vista a sense of family and permanence. After the turn of the century, wealthy entrepreneurs added style. In the meantime the civic-minded have always provided practicality. It remains now to explore those who contributed another sort of fame—painters, writers, scholars, actors—a variety of celebrated persons.

Alexander Stirling Calder, noted sculptor, was one of the first artists in Linda Vista, although he didn't stay long. Suffering from tuberculosis and "feeling the need of a wider impulse for his imagination," Calder left the East Coast for southern California and its promise of renewed health and inspiration.[1] Calder, his wife and two children lived for three years on Marengo Street in Pasadena before moving to a "barngalow" on Linda Vista Avenue where they stayed from 1908 to 1910.[2] Alexander, Calder's son and the inventor of the modern-day mobile, records many of the family's experiences in Linda Vista in his book, *Calder: An Autobiography with Pictures.*

The elder Calder executed one of his most famous works for

Throop Polytechnic Institute (later renamed the California Institute of Technology) after Pasadena architect Myron Hunt, a personal friend, recommended him for the job. Calder chiseled four panels and three arches for the school's new administration building exteriors, receiving a $5,000 remuneration.[3] The theme of these works is modern education, done in the French Beaux-Arts style studied by Calder while he attended school in Paris. David Starr Jordan, president of Stanford University, said of the Caltech work:

> Never has there been such a perfect combination of art and nature as in this work. . . Future generations will be amazed to find such an achievement in this city of the outermost western coast far removed from all art centers.[4]

After the 1971 earthquake, the Calder panels and arches were cut into forty-six pieces and placed in storage. Recently refurbished with funds provided by Dr. and Mrs. Arnold Beckman, the pieces are now reassembled and adorn the northern facade of the Arnold and Mabel Beckman Laboratory of Chemical Synthesis. Certain other preserved parts of the arches are contained in an adjacent courtyard.

When her husband was busy elsewhere, Nanette Calder, also an artist, used their Linda Vista studio to paint and sculpt. She also entered into community life and once coached and arranged an evening of "tableaux vivants" for the Valley Hunt Club, sort of a one-time Laguna Art Festival for Pasadena.

Declared cured of tuberculosis and finding southern California a bit too bucolic and unsophisticated for his tastes, Calder relocated to San Francisco in 1910, where he was "Sculptor-in-chief" for the 1915 Panama-Pacific International Exposition. After the exposition, the Calders moved to New York City. Calder's daughter later wrote, "My parents agreed with president Jordan that they were far removed from all [art] centers—too far."[5] But a trend had been established—artists in Linda Vista.

Linda Vista has its representatives of the "Eucalyptus School," a name sometimes used for an early twentieth-century southern California style of landscape painting. Trees silhouetted

Elmer Wachtel, California and western landscape artist. *Courtesy Huntington Library.*

against a pale blue sky, fields thick with poppies, the shady bend in a rocky Arroyo, hills dazzling with earth colors in full sun— these were some of the subjects that inspired the painters. Linda Vista artists moved "in the center of that group of 'Arroyo' painters which made early history."[6] Today, their works sometimes sell for thousands of dollars at art auctions.

Elmer and Marion Wachtel were two such "Eucalyptus" artists, and the account of their marriage has a storybook quality. As a young woman, Marion studied music in Paris and then moved to San Francisco to paint. When she planned a 1903 visit to Los Angeles, fellow artist and friend William Keith suggested she look up Elmer Wachtel, a violin-playing painter. This she did, and in two weeks they were engaged. But Marion had second thoughts about the pending marriage and fled to Chicago. Elmer followed and convinced her to return to California to marry him.

The couple established their first home and studio on Sichel Street in Highland Park, overlooking the Arroyo and near a number of artists. They then moved to Mount Washington, and in 1921 when that area became too populous, they sought the seclusion of Linda Vista, locating at 1155 Lida Street.[7]

Elmer Wachtel studied painting in New York and London before coming to California in 1882. He was one of the first painters to choose California and Western landscapes as his subject matter, instead of the more traditional European landscapes. Cultural historian Kevin Starr writes: "Possessed thoroughly by the spirit of the Arroyo, Wachtel wooed the wild landscape of his region..."[8] In addition to painting, Wachtel sculpted, carved furniture, designed cars, and once played first violin with the Los Angeles Philharmonic Orchestra.

Wachtel revealed himself as a bit of a philosopher when he wrote from Linda Vista to an ailing friend:

> It is not easy to get a focus on the mess one is wallowing in—and to me the busy hum is a mess. The busy, hurrying mob may look interested, but my opinion is that they are not so much interested as they are nervous. They all want money, but even those who want to can't stop after they get it. Being happy or unhappy is perhaps due more to the man than to material conditions and I think I can understand your being happy in spite of the cause of your exile [tuberculosis]."[9]

Together, the Wachtels painted and traveled throughout the Southwest, riding horseback, taking trips to the Sierras, and concentrating on desert and Indian scenes in Arizona and New Mexico. Their works were often exhibited in tandem. This mutual support of the other's work was cut short, however, when Elmer died in 1929 while he and Marion were painting in Mexico. After her husband's death, Marion continued to live in Linda Vista and to paint and exhibit. She died in 1954.

Orrin A. White, a textile designer from Illinois, moved to Pasadena, where he took up painting. He and his artist wife, Margaret White, commissioned Marston, Van Pelt and Mayberry to build them a home at 1205 Linda Vista Avenue.

White won many prizes for his landscape paintings and was a popular lecturer and instructor. He was one of the founders and a vice president of the Pasadena Society of Artists. Many considered him the "dean" of the Arroyo Seco school of painting, to which he commented, "I never heard of such a school."[10]

The early driveway and house of the James Scripps Booth residence, Marston and Van Pelt architects. *Courtesy Rockwell Family, Linda Vista Collection, Pasadena Historical Society.*

In 1961 White was accused of violating zoning codes by running an art school in his home. In a letter he convinced the superintendent of buildings that eight students once a week did not constitute a business.

James Scripps-Booth, artist and designer of the Scripps-Booth automobile, painted in California during the 1920s. Marston and Van Pelt designed a Mediterranean-style home for him in 1922 at what is now 1066 Charles Street. Writer Medora Clark, Booth's wife, describes their Linda Vista surroundings in a *California Southland* magazine article: "The green bank above is a mass of native chaparral and the open Arroyo bed gives a sense of space and freedom."[11]

No relation to Orrin White, Nona L. White was another Linda Vista landscape painter. She was part of the local art scene from 1925 to 1936, while living at 1134 Wabash Street. White was also an art critic, French and Spanish language tutor and designer of book and magazine covers. She once served as director of art at the South Pasadena Women's Club.

Sunlight on flower blossoms characterizes the painting of Frederick A. Zimmerman, who moved to 1180 Afton Street during the early 1930s and remained there until the 1940s. Unlike Elmer Wachtel, who avoided artists' organizations, Zimmerman enthusiastically involved himself with Pasadena art. He studied under the well-known local teacher Jean Mannheim, taught at the Pasadena Art Institute and presided over the Pasadena Society of Artists, with Orrin White on his board. Besides flowers, Zimmerman's favorite subjects were mountains and the San Pedro Harbor. He also did sculptures, miniatures and wood blocks.

Ruth Munson, an artist who lived for many years at 1445 Linda Ridge Road, is well known for her colorful and intimate garden scenes and for her portraits of such people as Dorothy Kirsten, Buckminster Fuller and Dr. Lee Dubridge. One of her paintings was used for the 1983 Pasadena Showcase House poster. In the late 1970s Munson decided that the new Art Center College of Design was too excellent and convenient an opportunity to pass up. Already an established painter, she nonetheless enrolled and graduated in 1979.

Painters and sculptors were not the only artists attracted to Linda Vista. Photographer Mabel Watson lived at 1389 Linda Vista Avenue in the 1920s while maintaining an art shop in Pasadena. Watson specialized in portrayals of children in gardens and in portraits—naturalist John Burroughs is one of her more famous subjects.

The architectural magazines of the 1920s and 1930s display advertisements of furniture and interior panelings designed and manufactured by Linda Vistan George S. Hunt. Hunt's furnishings, once the ultimate in prestige, are still found in private homes and Southland institutions such as Caltech, the Pasadena Civic Auditorium, and the William Andrews Clark Memorial Library of the University of California at Los Angeles. His pieces are often massive, yet have an intimacy because of his sensitive use of wood. Hunt carved most of his furniture at a small studio located at the intersection of California Boulevard and Arroyo Parkway in Pasadena.

Writers Fletcher and Winifred Dobyns, residents of Linda Vista during the 1930s, lived first at 1741 Linda Vista Avenue and then at 870 Chula Vista Avenue. Winifred, a landscape architect, lectured extensively about horticulture and published a volume entitled *California Gardens,* a collection of photographs of memorable gardens throughout the state.

Fletcher Dobyns, a Harvard graduate and attorney from Chicago, focused on cleaning up political corruption. A legal scholar, he wrote several books, including *An Expose of the Power of Propaganda. Cases on Criminal Law and Procedure: Justice Holmes and the Fourteenth Amendment.* He served as attorney general of Illinois and assistant attorney general of the United States. Dobyns and his wife came to the Pasadena area in 1925, and he practiced law with the Los Angeles firm of Latham and Watkins. Dobyns died in 1942.

Stuart and Elizabeth Pickett Chevalier, both writers, moved from New York City in 1938 to 1065 Charles Street in Linda Vista, where they lived until 1950. Wellesley-educated and heir to her father's Kentucky tobacco property, Elizabeth Chevalier wrote the novel *Drivin' Woman,* a story about a Virginia belle, a river-boat gambler and the tobacco business after the Civil War— Chevalier was always concerned about the conflict between agrarianism and the new industrialism. She also wrote several books on the Red Cross, for which she actively worked. She was an associate producer and writer of the 1923 film *Redskin,* starring Tom Mix; a trustee of the Westridge School for Girls; an outspoken advocate of human rights and a feminist. Not one to mince words, she commented during an interview with the Junior League about her up-beat outlook on life: "A fresh egg is just as real as a rotten egg and a lot more pleasant to eat."[12]

A polio victim as a child in Kentucky, Stuart Chevalier was crippled for the rest of his life. An attorney as well as a writer, his book *A Window on Broadway* is a collection of personal essays in which he encourages readers to make each day productive and vital. He also wrote and published *The United Nations: Its First Six Years, War's End and After* and *The World Charter and the*

Road to Peace. Chevalier was program chairman for the Pasadena Twilight Club, a private educational organization for men, and he and Elizabeth were trustees of Occidental College. In 1957 she endowed the Chevalier Chair of Diplomacy in memory of her husband, who had recently died.

Colonel John Judson Poole, author and collector of American Indian artifacts, lived at 1002 Linda Vista Avenue. Poole graduated from the United States Military Academy at West Point, once served as an aide to President Theodore Roosevelt, and was honorably retired from the service in 1919. He owned an interest in Midwestern iron ore before coming to Pasadena after World War I. Poole was connected with Pasadena's Security First National Bank. He financed a new wing of the Southwest Museum in 1939 and donated his collection of Indian baskets from 112 different tribes. He wrote a book entitled *American Cavalcade* about his family's history. Poole died in 1940.

Dr. Frederick Webb Hodge, an ethnologist and pioneer of American anthropology who lived for over twenty years at 1375 Lida Street, is one of the most well-remembered Linda Vista scholars. Born in Plymouth, England, he was educated at George Washington University, Pomona College and the University of Mexico.

Scholarly pursuits were Hodge's way of life. He helped found the American Anthropological Association and was director of the Southwest Museum from 1931 to 1956. Hodge was also a member of the United States Geological Survey, the Southern Archaeological Expedition, the executive boards of the Smithsonian Institute, the Bureau of American Ethnology, and the New York Museum of the American Indian. He edited a two-volume work, *Handbook of American Indians North of Mexico,* and other publications on archaeology and native people. A bibliography of his writing lists more than 350 works.

Hodge felt strongly that traditional Indian legends were often verifiable. One such legend that he defended along with his friend Charles Lummis, southern California writer, told of an Indian village named the Enchanted Mesa, built on top of New

Dr. Frederick Webb Hodge, pioneer of American anthropology. *Courtesy Pasadena Historical Society.*

Mexico's 430 foot high Katsimo. When a Princeton archaeologist claimed to have established the legend as incorrect by spending three hours on the mesa top searching futilely for artifacts, Hodge was unbelieving and went to the site himself. He spent twenty-four hours on the summit and discovered numerous relics that he felt proved his point. His friend A.C. Vroman, Pasadena book dealer, went on the trip with him and recorded the finds with photographs. Returning to Linda Vista, Hodge wrote an article declaring the Princeton scholar's published account of no consequence.

Southwest writer Mary Austin was a personal friend of Hodge and his wife, Zahrah, sharing their love of Indian artifacts. In a 1932 letter to Austin, Hodge invited her to visit them at their home in Linda Vista:

a charming Monterey-Spanish one-story house, surrounded by a garden with a white picket fence, the whole set down on a green hillside amid an old apricot orchard which has just turned green after a marvelous blossom time.[13]

Hodge continued working until a few days before his death in 1956.

Dr. Chester Stock, a scholar of fossils, lived at 1633 Linda Vista Avenue. Stock was a member of the National Academy of Sciences, curator of paleontology for the Los Angeles County Museum, professor of paleontology at Caltech and president of the Geological Society of America. He focused on the mammalian paleontology of western North America and published extensively.

Jeane Daniel Gunder of 310 Linda Vista Avenue during the 1940s studied the evolution and metamorphasis of moths and butterflies. Highly-esteemed in his field, he owned extensive collections of lepidoptera and contributed frequently to entomological journals.

Clark B. Millikan, son of physicist and Nobel Prize winner Robert A. Millikan, lived during the 1950s at 1500 Normandy Drive. Millikan was on the Caltech faculty for thirty-seven years and became a foremost pioneer in aerospace research and development. He also served as chairman of the Board of Directors of the Jet Propulsion Laboratory.

Princeton-educated John Willis Baer, president of Occidental College from 1906 to 1916, and his wife, Lora, lived at 809 Linda Vista Avenue from 1918 until his retirement a few years later, when they moved to Pasadena's Huntington Hotel. After stepping down from his post at Occidental, Baer went into banking and served as vice president of the Union National Bank of Pasadena. He was always active in church work and took leading positions in several Presbyterian general assemblies.

Besides artists, writers and scholars, other celebrated persons have lived in Linda Vista. Perhaps the best known is Charles Paddock, one-time Olympic gold medal sprinter. Texas-born Paddock moved with his family to Pasadena in 1907 and attended

Polytechnic Elementary School, Pasadena High School, the University of Southern California and the University of Paris, where he received the degree of doctor of philosophy. He and his wife lived at 985 Linda Vista Avenue. Paddock's athletic achievements brought him many honors: champion state high school sprinter, holder of 94 world records for short-distance running, 10-time American sprint champion and winner of the 100-meter run in the 1920 Olympics.

Paddock entered the newspaper business while still a young man and served at one time or another as vice president and general manager of the Pasadena Star News Publishing Company, as publisher of the *Star News* and *Pasadena Post* and as business manager of the Long Beach Press-Telegram Publishing Company. Besides his involvement in athletics and journalism, Paddock lectured widely and authored two books, *The Fastest Human* (1932) and *Track and Field* (1933). During World War II he took a leave of absence from newspaper work to accept a captain's commission in the Marine Corps. In 1943 while on duty, the forty-two year old Paddock died in an Alaska plane crash. Caltech's athletic field is named in his honor.

Dr. Pierce's Pleasant Purgative Pellets was the colorful name given to physician Valentine Mott Pierce's manufactured remedies, a formula inherited from his inventor father. The name of the family business was World's Dispensary Medical Association until Pierce changed it to Pierce's Proprietaries, Inc. A resident during the 1930s of 200 Fern Drive, Pierce had other interests than purgative pellets. He was involved in real estate (Alabama Land Development Company), glass bottling (Pierce Glass Company of Pennsylvania), coal and lumber (Pierce Coal and Lumber Company of Alabama), and natural gas (Pierce Natural Gas Company of Pennsylvania). He also owned a one-third interest in tiny Saint Vincent's Island in the Gulf of Mexico. Pierce died in Pasadena in 1942.

Ollie Prickett, actor and long-time resident of Banyan Street, remembers riding his bicycle from Pasadena through the Arroyo Seco to pick wild apricots in Linda Vista. In the Arroyo during the depression, a camp housing itinerants was burned by city officials because of a fear of smallpox epidemic. Most of all, he recalls his experiences as one of the founders of the Pasadena Playhouse.[14]

President of the first Pasadena High School class to graduate in the Rose Bowl, Prickett was later active in the Tournament of Roses Association. He was always involved with the inner workings of the Linda Vista community and recollects the evening during World War II when the Long Beach bombing scare occurred. All of the Linda Vista men serving as air raid wardens donned helmets and dashed around the streets to see that all lights were turned off.

Like his brother Oliver ("Ollie"), Charles Prickett was a Linda Vista resident and Pasadena Playhouse founder. Charles' wife, Maudie, an actress and one of Hollywood's first female comedians, once played Jack Benny's secretary. After Charles died, she married C. Bernard Cooper, Linda Vista resident and mayor of Pasadena.

Actor Victor Jory and his wife, actress Jean Innes, lived in a Paul Williams house at 111 Linda Vista Avenue in the 1930s and 1940s. Innes once played Ramona to Jory's Alessandro at the Ramona Pageant in Hemet. Jory also directed the play. As an actor Jory's credits list parts in the films *Tom Sawyer* and *Gone with the Wind*. An "evil-eyed heavy" is the way Prickett affectionately describes the movie roles most often portrayed by Jory.

C. Bernard Cooper was not the only Pasadena mayor to live in Linda Vista. Architect and one-time mayor Mortimer J. ("Tim") Matthews designed a family home for Linda Ridge Road. Mayor John Crowley and his family live in a 1904 Tudor-style house on Linda Vista Avenue.

Creative persons continue to live on the slopes west of the Rose Bowl, still attracted by the same rustic elements that brought artist Calder to the community and still contributing to Linda Vista's distinct personality.

CHAPTER EIGHT

Architecture and Homes

On the whole, Linda Vista is a very favored section which is showing and will continue to show
rapid progress and development in high class
homes of refinement.

Pasadena *Star News,*
September 2, 1922

Linda Vista has retained a rural atmosphere despite its proximity to cities. Streets have little traffic. The moat-like Arroyo
makes freeways seem farther away than they are. Dense natural
growth absorbs noise, and a sense of removal from metropolitan
life lingers.

Travelers here find routes that wind, twist and loop. Some
roads are still lined with boulders brought up from the Arroyo
over a half-century ago. A few pepper trees remain from the Park
Nursery days. Oaks and elms, with top branches intertwined,
create shaded tunnels out of certain streets. Hard-to-find lanes
end at rugged ravines. The whole is a unique preserve, seemingly
unperturbed by the humans around it.

Tract developments in Linda Vista date back to 1887 when
the Linda Vista Land Company first sold lots to arriving settlers.
Developers eventually reached their most elaborate schemes
with the Pegfair Estates and El Mirador developments.

Many of the area's architectural styles reflect the Arts and
Crafts Movement of the early 1900s, spearheaded by Pasadenan
George Wharton James and his Arroyo Craftsman Guild and
rooted in the philosophies of Englishmen John Ruskin and William Morris. (Interestingly, in 1920 the Pasadena *Evening Post*
reported the purchase by James of thirty acres of property along

"Spend your life on the verandah," by Elmer Wachtel, depicts an ideal and early twentieth-century life in Linda Vista. *Courtesy Huntington Library.*

Linda Vista Avenue for a studio for poet and friend Charles M. Crocker, but he seems never to have built it.)[1] With its focus on the hand-made, one-of-a-kind object, the movement was best served by an idealism which looked back in history and which a rural setting seemed best able to satisfy. Such aestheticism found a receptive following along the Arroyo and in Linda Vista.

Not all noteworthy homes on the slopes have been large: a 1925 Marston, Van Pelt and Maybury house at 2273 Parkview Avenue won first prize in the House Beautiful Publishing Company contest for best small house design of the previous three years west of the Mississippi.

Craftsman architecture is most ideally represented in Pasadena by the designs of the Greene brothers, Charles Sumner and Henry Mather. Several examples of their bungalow homes, a mingling of the California shingle style and Japanese influence, shoulder the western bank of the Arroyo on property once belonging to Nathan Yocum's Park Place Tract. Although the Greenes designed no homes in Linda Vista, their influence is felt in a number of its homes.

A plethora of designs exist in Linda Vista structures. The Mediterranean look shows southern California's effort to emulate things Italian. Wallace Neff, whose concerns bridged both the nineteenth and twentieth centuries, created dream houses of European styles. The chalet, with its hand-hewn quality, is a Craftsman effort by Constantine Hillman and represented by Bavarian hunting lodges on Mira Vista Terrace. Fowler's Andalusian farmhouse on Las Palmas features a central patio and cactus garden that lie in the shadows of the Ventura Freeway arches, and his Mallorcan farmhouse on El Circulo is also other worldly. Conrad Buff III fashioned a "Southwest Classic" made of teak, stucco, redwood and quarry lime for the family residence on Wicks Road.[2] David A. Ogilvie's Tudor villa on La Vereda Road is grounded in tradition. By contrast, modern glass and post and beam houses reach back to a philosophy extolling simplicity and functionalism, and stark rectangular cubicles rise up from wooded lots.

The list of styles and architects goes on—Queen Anne, Miesian, Gothic, Mission, colonial, modular. Test, Ellwood, Ain, Hensman, Matthews, Eggers, Evison, Kucera. And more. Linda Vista is an architectural refuge, and exploring its streets offers a study of contrasts.

The environment of the slopes that at one time sheltered the Indians has fortunately not eroded into a metropolitan maze of cramped lots, crowded streets and blocked views. Nature is preserved amidst the homes of the moderns. Both the historic perspective and natural terrain reside here.

Acknowledgments

Many people encouraged and helped me in this endeavor, but unfortunately I can mention here only a few. Jean Owen gave me the idea; Hank Silka, my editor, provided patience and exacting standards, and friends and colleagues at the Huntington Library and elsewhere gave added assistance. My mother, Vivian Burke, and my three children, David, Larry and Marcia Wayte, were always ready with valuable moral support.

I have been fortunate to have access to the following institutions: Honnold Library of the Claremont University Center; Huntington Library in San Marino; Pasadena Historical Society; Pasadena Public Library; Southwest Museum Library, Sherman Library in Corona del Mar, and the UCLA Research Library. To the Huntington Library I owe a special thanks for so generously giving of desk space, staff assistance and their extensive local history collections.

Finally, my appreciation goes to the Historical Society of Southern California, to the editor of its *Southern California Quarterly,* Doyce B. Nunis, Jr., and to its executive director, Thomas F. Andrews, who first envisioned my work as a book and saw it through to that end.

Notes

Introduction.

[1]Pasadena Planning Department, *City of Pasadena Area Analysis Study 1960-1980,* October 1983, p. 1.

[2]Charles Frederick Holder, *All About Pasadena and Its Vicinity* (Boston: Lee and Shepard, 1889), p. 23.

Chapter One.

[1]Hiram Reid, *History of Pasadena* (Pasadena: Pasadena Historical Society, 1895), p. 27.

[2]Al Carr letters, Pasadena Files, Pasadena Public Library.

[3]Bernice Eastman Johnston, "Gabrielino Indians of San Gabriel: The Great Valleys in the American Period," *Masterkey,* XXXI (November-December 1957): 187-188.

[4]Robert Glass Cleland, *Cattle on a Thousand Hills: Southern California 1850-1880* (San Marino: Huntington Library, 1941), pp. 18-19.

[5]Robert Glass Cleland, "The Twilight Cavalcade 1895-1945," address, Twilight Club, October 16, 1945, Pasadena, p. 3.

[6]Cleland, *Cattle,* p. 20.

[7]Cleland, "Twilight," p. 3.

[8]June Dougherty, "History," in *La Canada: A Look at Our Community* (La Canada Unit, League of Women Voters of Pasadena, 1973).

[9]Joseph Lancaster Brent, "Life in California," annotated by Frances Rosella (Kenner) Brent, 1900, Joseph L. Brent Collection, Huntington Library, p. 23.

[10]Horace Bell, *Reminiscences of a Ranger* (Santa Barbara: Wallace Hebbard, 1927), p. 372.

[11]W.W. Robinson, *Maps of Los Angeles: From Ord's Survey of 1849 to the End of the Boom of the Eighties* (Los Angeles: Dawson's Bookshop, 1966), p. 25.

Chapter Two.

[1]Benjamin Dreyfus letters to Cave Johnson Couts, January 29, 1874 and July 13, 1869, Manuscript Collection, Huntington Library.

[2]J.C. Sherer, *Glendale and Vicinity* (Glendale: Glendale History Publishing Company, 1922), p. 53.

[3]Ibid.

[4]David C. Le Shana, *Quakers in California* (Newburg: The Barclay Press, 1969), p. 108.

[5]Los Angeles County Hall of Records, Deed Book No. 91, page 130, July 5, 1882.

[6]Reid, *History of Pasadena,* p. 348.

[7]Los Angeles *Evening Express,* May 3, 1886.

[8]Blanche Dorn manuscript.

[9]Robert H. Peterson, *Altadena's Golden Years* (Alhambra: Sinclair Painting and Lithography Incorporated, 1976), p. 76.

[10]Evidence of Clark's having at least one milking cow is found in the 1890-1910 "Pasturage Records" of the San Rafael Rancho Company. Clark is listed as paying $5.00 to Mr. Rust in 1892 for grazing privileges for a seven-month heifer. These records are a part of the San Rafael Rancho Company Collection at the Huntington Library.

[11]Pasadena *Daily Union,* December 31, 1887.

[12]*Pasadena and Valley Union,* March 29, 1884.

[13]J.W. Wood, *Pasadena: Historical and Personal* (N.p.: n.p., 1917), p. 103.

[14]Pasadena *Daily Union,* December 31, 1887.

[15]Pasadena *Weekly Union,* December 3, 1887.

[16]Reid, *History of Pasadena,* p. 374.

[17]Los Angeles *Evening Express,* May 13, 1886.

[18]Pasadena *Daily Union,* October 7, 1887.

[19]C.F. Shoop article, Pasadena *Star News,* July 8, 1951.

[20]Shoop, Pasadena *Star News,* March 12, 1937.

[21]Pasadena *Daily Union,* January 27, 1888.

[22]Ibid., December 31, 1887.

[23]Ibid., January 4, 1888.

[24]T.D. Allin, "John Brown" manuscript, (May 17, 1934), Pasadena Historical Society.

[25]Al Carr letters.

Chapter Three.

[1]Harold D. Carew, *History of the San Gabriel Valley, California* (Clarke Publishing Company, 1930), I:323.

[2]Glenn S. Dumke, *The Boom of the Eighties in Southern California* (San Marino: Huntington Library, 1970), pp. 259-260.

[3]Pasadena *Daily Union,* September 15, 1887.

[4]Ibid., October 13, 1887.

[5]Los Angeles *Times,* October 17, 1887.

[6]Pasadena *Daily Union,* October 31, 1887.

[7]Ibid., January 4, 1988.

[8]Ibid.

[9]Reid, *History of Pasadena,* p. 307.

[10]Pasadena *Daily News,* June 26, 1902.

[11]California Criminal Case No. C7555, Superior Court Archives, Los Angeles.

[12]Letter, A.D. Yocum to Major Ward Lamon, May 20, 1886, Manuscript Collection, Huntington Library.

[13]Pasadena *Daily News,* June 26, 1902.

[14]Los Angeles County Death Records: Hannah Yocum, Los Angeles County Archives.

[15]California Superior Court, May 4, 1917, Petition for Probate of Will: John D. Yocum, Los Angeles.

Chapter Four.

[1]1900 United States Census Records, Mormon Genealogical Library, Los Angeles.

[2]Schoonmaker biography file, Pasadena Public Library.

Chapter Five.
[1]"Builders of Mountain Roads," *California Southland,* No. 5, 1919, p. 17.
[2]Pasadena *Star News,* May 13, 1916.
[3]Ibid., December 15, 1911.
[4]Ibid., June 13, 1925.
[5]Ibid., December 1, 1911.
[6]Ibid., September 27, 1924.
[7]Ibid., April 12, 1939.

Chapter Six
[1]Today, the Linda Vista School still maintains a small-town ambiance, even though many of its students are bussed. A good example of the school's community spirit is the recent collaboration between the school and the Art Center College of Design in the production of a pictorial history book of Linda Vista in commemoration of the school's 1988 centennial.
[2]Shoop, Pasadena *Star News,* July 15, 1951.
[3]Reid, *History of Pasadena,* p. 187.
[4]Shoop, Pasadena *Star News,* May 31, 1953.
[5]Pasadena *Daily News,* March 23, 1908.
[6]Peterson, *Altadena,* p. 84.
[7]Pasadena *Daily News,* September 2, 1910.
[8]Pasadena *Star News,* August 13, 1914.
[9]Ibid., December 11, 1924.
[10]Grace J. Oberbeck, *History of La Crescenta-La Canada Valleys* (Montrose: The Ledger, 1938), p. 28.
[11]"History of the Linda Vista Branch Library" (Pasadena Public Library, 1981), p. 2.
[12]Pasadena *Star News,* March 30, 1973.
[13]Los Angeles *Times,* March 14, 1976.

Chapter Seven
[1]Charles Hanson Towne, "Sculptors of the Southwest," *Craftsman,* May 1915, pp. 149-155.
[2]Margaret Calder Hayes, *Three Alexander Calders* (Middlebury: Paul S. Ericksson, 1977), p. 38.
[3]Micheline Vogt, "The Calder Arches" (California Institute of Technology Architectural Committee, 1986).
[4]Hayes, *Calders,* p. 134.
[5]Ibid., p. 135.
[6]Elmer Wachtel, Biographical Files, Pasadena Public Library.
[7]Nancy Dustin Wall Moure, *Dictionary of Art and Artists in Southern California before 1930* (Glendale: Dustin Publications, 1975), pp. 262-263.
[8]Kevin Starr, *Inventing the Dream* (New York: Oxford University Press, 1985), p. 121.
[9]Elmer Wachtel letter to Charles Dwight Willard, December 1925, Manuscript Collection, Huntington Library.
[10]Orrin White, Biographical Files, Pasadena Public Library.
[11]Medora Clark, "European Landscape Versus California," *California Southland,* February 1923, p. 9.

[12]Pasadena Junior League, *Community News,* Pasadena, 1953.

[13]Frederick Webb Hodge letter to Mary Austin, March 18, 1932, Austin Collection, Huntington Library.

[14]Ollie Prickett, personal interview with the author, November 1986, Pasadena and telephone call, October 28, 1990.

Chapter Eight

[1]Pasadena *Evening Post,* April 19, 1920.

[2]Los Angeles *Times,* February 1, 1981.

Index

Adams, Edward A., 76
Afflect, Veta, 50, 68-69
Agar, James, 67
Ain, Gregory, 95
Allin, T.D., 33
Altadena: naming of, 26; 29
Anaheim, 19, 21-22, 25, 26
Angeles Mesa Co., 63
Annandale, 5, 57, 70
Armour, M. Cochrane, 57-60, 64, 79
Arndt, Mr. and Mrs. Howard, 66
Arroyo Craftsman Guild, 93
Arroyo Seco, 9, 10, 11; and Rancho San
    Rafael, 16, 23; and Clark, 26, 28; Scoville
    property, 34-35; as an outing spot, 35-36,
    69, 72; and the Eucalyptus School, 83, 85,
    91-92, 93
Art Center College of Design: and Dumm
    property, 65-66, 72; founding of, 76-78, 86
Associated Charities of Pasadena, 70
Austin, Mary, 89

Baer, John Willis, 90
Baer, Lora, 90
Ball, Benjamin F., 23, 43
Bandini, Arturo, 36
Batchelder, Ernest A., 65
Beaudry, Prudent, 17, 19
Beckman, Dr. and Mrs. Arnold, 82
Bennet and Haskell, 61
Berraros (early resident), 49
Berriz (family), 49
Bird, Mrs. F.M., 71
Blankenhorn Realty, 62
Borie (buys La Cañada property), 15
Boston Building (Pasadena), 61
Brent, Joseph Lancaster, 15-17
Brookside Park, 31, 60
Brown, David, 78
Buff, Conrad, III, 95

Burbank, 11, 16
Burson, Lydia, 67
Busch Gardens, 58

Cabrillo, Juan Rodrigtuez, 5
Calder, Alexander, 81
Calder, Alexander Stirling, 81-82, 92
Calder: An Autobiography with Pictures, 81
Calder, Nanette, 82
California Institute of Technology, 64;
    "demolition experts," 71-72, 82, 86, 90, 91
California Olive Company, 26
California Southland, 56, 85
Carew, Harold D., 37
Carmelita, 34
Carr, Al, 10, 36
Carr, Jeanne, 10, 24, 36
Carr, Ezra, 10, 24, 36
Carson, John, 49
Carson, Robert, 29
Cattle on a Thousand Hills (Cleland), 13
Central Building (Pasadena), 61
Chamberlain (family), 34, 64
Chandler, Harry, 63
Channing, Grace Ellery, 30
Chapin, Mrs. Lon F., 69
Chapman, Alfred Beck, 17, 19
Chesebrough, F.P., 63
Chevalier, Elizabeth Pickett, 87-88
Chevalier, Stuart, 87-88
Chevalier Chair of Diplomacy, 88
Childs, O.W., 17
Childs Tract, 17
City Directory (Pasadena), 71, 73
Clark, Byron, 24-27, 28, 29; and pepper trees,
    36, 41; leaves Linda Vista, 43, 44, 67
Clark, Medora, 85
Claudio (legendary character), 46
Cleland, Robert Glass, 13
Clifford, J.P., 63

Codrick, W.C., 71
Colorado River Aqueduct Association, 64
Colorado Street bridge, 35, 71
Congar, Orville H., 24
Cooper, C. Bernard, 92
Corey (family), 49
Coronel, Ignacio, 14-15
Costa (early resident), 49
Crocker, Charles M., 94
Crosby, George Howard, 58-59
Crowley, John, 92
Crown Transfer and Storage Company
     (Pasadena), 61

Day, Clarence, 56
Devil's Gate (and dam), 23, 24, 71
Dix (family), 49
Dixon, William, 71
Dobbins, Horace M., 62
Dobyns, Fletcher, 87
Dobyns, Winifred, 87
Dominguez, Juan Jose, 11
Dorn, Arthur, 45, 46
Dorn, Blanche, 45, 46
Dorn, Joseph, 49
Dorn, Richard, 45, 49, 67
Dreyfus, Benjamin, 19, 21, 43
Dreyfuss, John, 77
Dumm, Margaret, 65
Dumm, Wesley I., 65-66, 77, 79

Eagle Rock, 19, 21
Eggers, Henry, 95
Elevated cycleway, 62
Elias, Jacob, 17
Elliott, Whitt, 36
Ellwood, Craig, and Associates, 77, 95
Elsinore, 38, 41
El Mirador Dairy, 52
El Mirador Ranch, 50-52, 56, 78
Enchanted Mesa (Katsimo), 89-90
Entrepreneurs, 6, 53, 55-56, 64
Eucalyptus School, 82
Evison, Leland, 95

Fages, Pedro, 11
First National Bank of Pasadena, 63

First Trust and Savings Bank of Pasadena,
     63
First Universalist Church of Pasadena, 30
Fiscus, Marshall D., 34, 64
Fiscus, Mrs. Marshall, 69
Flint, Frank P., 73
Flintridge, 62, 73
Flintridge Biltmore Hotel, 73
Flintridge Boulevard, 73
Flintridge Sacred Heart Academy, 24, 74
Flynn, Thomas F., 31, 41
Flora (native), 6, 7
Ford, Freeman, 56
Fowler, Edward M., 62-63, 95
Fowler, Edward Payson, 62-63
Fowler-Modisette Realty Co., 63
Franciscan missionaries, 5-6, 9
Fruit crystallization plant (1886), 27

Gabrielino Indians, 9, 10, 12
Glassell, Andrew, 17
Glendale, 11, 17, 22
Gold mining (in the Linda Vista area), 36
Gradow, George, 66
Great Partition of 1871, 19
Green Hotel, 62, 64
Greene, Charles Sumner, 59, 94
Greene, Henry, 59, 94
Griffith Park, 17
Griggs, Mrs., 29, 49
Gunder, Jeane Daniel, 90

Hall, John B., 63
Hall, Peter, 59
Halstead, S. Hazard, 70
Hamlin, Mary J., 58
Hand laundry (Linda Vista), 71
Hayes, Benjamin, 15
Heald, Frank, 33, 34
Helky, C.T., 49
Hensman, Donald, 95
Hillman, J. Constantine, 58, 59, 95
Hodge, Frederick Webb, 88-90
Hodge, Jacob, 29, 34, 57
Hodge, Zahrah, 89
Hodgkins, H., 22
Hoffman family: Dorothy Brown, 53;

Eleanore, 50, 51; George, 50, 51; Halleck, 50, 51; James, 50, 51; Marjorie, 50; Paul, 50-53; Virginia, 50
Hoffman ranch, 50, 51, 78
Holder, Charles Frederick, 7
Holly Street bridge, 32, 57
Honnald Library, 60
Hopkins, C.T., 38
House Beautiful Publishing Co., 94
Hudson (family), 49
Hunt, George S., 86
Hunt, Myron, 60, 82
Huntington Hotel, 63, 68, 90
Huntington Memorial Hospital, 34

Indiana Colony, 36
Indian Flat (as early name for Linda Vista), 9, 10, 24
Innes, Jean, 92

James, George Wharton, 93
Jensen, J.M., 30, 62, 70
Jet Propulsion Laboratory, 90
Johnston, Bernice Eastman, 10
Jordan, David Starr, 82
Jory, Victor, 92
Jumbo Knob (hill between Linda Vista and Annandale), 23, 31, 34, 60, 62
Junior League of Pasadena, 87
Junior Philharmonic of Pasadena, 66
Jurgensen, Harold, 74
Jurgensen's Market, 74-75

Kealey, T.S., 52
Keith, William, 83
Kellogg, L.G., 26, 28, 41
Kendall, Bella Otis, 60-61
Kinney-Kendall Building (Pasadena), 61
Kubly, Donald, 77-78
Kucera, Joseph, 95

La Cañada, 14, 55
La Cañada atras de Los Berdugos, 14
"Ladies Trail," 36
Lake Vineyard Land and Water Association, 23
Lamon, Ward H., 42

Land titles (1851), 15
Latham and Watkins, 87
La Vina Sanitarium, 70
Lemocher, G., 49
Lincoln, Abraham, 42
Lincoln, Mary Todd, 42
Linda Rosa (San Diego County), 31
Linda Vista: Area analysis study (1960-1980), 6-7; naming of, 24; as outing spot, 35-36; 1900 census records, 46-49; fire, 49; health camp, 70; annexation with Annandale and San Rafael, 28, 61-62, (1914) 70; street numbering, 70; early bus service, 71; street improvements (1924), 73; population (1946), 75; zoning, 78; street landscaping, 79
Linda Vista-Annandale Association, 74, 78, 79
Linda Vista Bridge, 23, 32, 35, 36, 50, 57, 58; as West Pasadena Railway bridge, 71, 72, 73
Linda Vista Fire Department, 74, 75
Linda Vista Friends of the Library, 75
Linda Vista Hotel, 28; as Carson Hotel, 29; as "Pepper Pot," 29, 32, 49
Linda Vista Land and Improvement Association, 49, 67, 68, 73
Linda Vista Library, 75-76
Linda Vista Neighborhood Association: (1924) 73, 74
Linda Vista School PTA, 69, 76
Linda Vista School, 10, 67-69; as Andrew Jackson School, 67-68; as William Cullen Bryant School, 68; as Sunday school, 69, 74, 75, 99n
Linda Vista streets: Afton Street, 86; Banyan Street, 91; Bryant Street, 68; Charles Street, 85, 87; Chula Vista Avenue, 87; El Circulo, 95; El Mirador Drive, 50; Fern Drive, 91; Holly Street, 73; Holly Vista Drive, 59; Inverness Drive, 26, 27, 29; La Vista Place, 29, 49; Las Palmas Road, 63, 95; La Vereda Road, 95; Lida Street, 10, 24, 29, 45, 63, 66, 72, 73, 83, 88; Linda Ridge, 86, 92; Linda Vista Avenue, 23, 26, 29, 59, 61, 63, 64, 70, 71, 72, 73, 74, 75, 81, 86, 87, 88, 90, 91, 92; Los Altos Drive, 60;

Mira Vista Terrace, 58, 95; Myrtle Street, 30; Normandy Lane, 62; Ontario Avenue, 29, 45, 46; Parkview Avenue, 29; Wellington Avenue, 29, 64, 68, 75; Wicks Road, 95
Linda Vistans, 75
Linnard, Daniel M., 63-64, 72
Lloyd, P.W., 49
Lopez, Encarnacion, 11
Los Angeles Evening Express, 24, 30
Los Angeles Times, 39, 77
Los Angeles and San Gabriel Valley Railroad, 30, 33
Lucerne (San Diego County), 33, 41
Lummis, Charles, 88-89

MacAdam, Isabel, 68
MacCormick Farm, 57
MacCoy, John, 38
Mannheim, Jean, 86
Maps of Los Angeles (Robinson), 19
Marston and Van Pelt, 85
Marston, Van Pelt, and Mayberry, 94
Mason, William S., 60
Masterkey (Southwest Museum), 10
Matthews, Mortimer J., 92, 95
Metropolitan Water District Aqueduct, 64
Mexican-American War, 15
Mexican Independence, 14
Micheltorena, Manuel, 14
Mies Van Der Rohe, Ludwig, 77
Millard Canyon, 26
Millard Canyon Water Co., 26
Millikan, Clark B., 90
Millikan, Robert A., 90
Mills, Mrs. C.E., 69
Mission San Fernando, 12
Mission San Gabriel, 6, 9, 10
Modisette, Robert M., 63, 64
Monk Hill, 23, 24, 25
Moreno, Al, 78
Morris, William, 93
Mossholder, Edith, 69
Mossholder (family), 45
Mount Lowe Incline Railway, 40, 56
Mountain View Cemetery, 42, 43
Mount Washington, 83

Muir, John, 24
Mundell, I.N., 31, 41
Municipal Improvement Act of 1915, 73
Munson, Ruth, 86

National Bank of Pasadena, 61
Neff, Wallace, 62, 95
Newell, Kenneth, 63
Newmark (family), 74
Nieto, Manuel, 11
Normandy, W.F., 62

Occidental College, 12, 90
Ogden, H.W., 31, 41
Ogilvie, David, 59, 95
Ojai Capital, 75
Olivewood Tract, 38

Pacific Coast Builders Conference, 79
Paddock, Charles, 90-91
Painter, John H., 23
Panama-Pacific International Exposition of 1915, 82
Park Nursery (also Park Place Nursery), 7, 26, 27, 32-33, 67, 93
Park Place Improvement Co., 31
Park Place Tract (also Park Place), 31, 32-33, 37, 40, 43, 95
Pasadena, 10, 21, 22, 32; turn-of-the-century, 55-56; Brookside Park, 60; 1895 map, 61; and annexation, 28, 61-62, 70; and street improvements, 73
Pasadena Art Institute, 86
Pasadena Art Museum, 66, 77
Pasadena Board of Directors, 64
Pasadena Board of Trade, 30, 64
Pasadena Chamber of Commerce, 63
Pasadena Daily, 33
Pasadena Daily News, 39, 40, 42, 70
Pasadena Daily Union, 27, 40, 55
Pasadena Evening Post, 93
Pasadena Evening Star, 49
Pasadena Garfield Child Study Circle, 69
Pasadena High School, 91, 92
Pasadena Ice Co., 56, 70
Pasadena Park Tract Land and Water Co., 31
Pasadena Planning Commission, 7

Pasadena Playhouse, 92
Pasadena Post, 91
Pasadena Public Library, 75
Pasadena School District, 67-68
Pasadena Society of Artists, 84, 85
Pasadena Star, 61
Pasadena Star News, 64, 77, 91
Pasadena, Star News Publishing Co., 91
Pasadena Theater Company, 71
Pasadena YMCA, 61
Pederson, John, 64
Pegfair, 29, 34; as Hillcrest, 64; as Fairview, 64-66, 75
Pegfair Estates, 65, 77, 78, 93
Philbrook, Emile Heseldon, 33
Pierce, Valentine Mott, 91
Pierson, George, 29, 49
Pletsch, Theodore, 74
Polytechnic Elementary School, 91
Pomona College, 60, 88
Poole, John Judson, 88
Portola, Gaspar de, 5, 6, 9
Prickett, Charles, 92
Prickett, Maudie, 92
Prickett, Oliver ("Ollie"), 91-92
Prosser (family), 49
Prosser, Mrs. Ralph, 69

Rancho de la Sierra de los Berdugos, 16
Rancho Encino, 13
Rancho Linda Vista, 57
Rancho San Pasqual, 16
Rancho San Rafael, 6, 11-14, 16, 19, 22
Real estate "boom" in southern California (1886-1888), 30-31
Real estate "bust" in southern California (1888-1889), 37-38
Receiving Hospital and Surgical Institute, 34
Reid, Hiram, 10
Reid, Hugo, 10
Reidebach, Henry, 49
Reservoir Hill (Pasadena), 23, 31
Reyes, Francisco, 12-13
Rheinschild, Bill, 78
Richards, Arabella, 64
Richards, Robert J., 64
Riggins, James A., 27

Robinson, W.W., 19
Romero, Maria de Jesus, 13
Rose Bowl, 79, 92
Rose Parade (see Tournament of Roses)
Ruhman, Mrs. R., 69
Rush, Judson, 56
Ruskin, John, 93

Salter, J., 59
Sanborn, H.T., 28
San Marino, 21
San Rafael (Pasadena), 19, 62, 70
San Rafael Improvement Co., 60
Santa Fe Railroad Co., 30
Sawtelle, Charles A., 41
Schibler, Hiram, 49
Schoonmaker, Reverend Ralph M., 49, 70
Schoonmaker, Mrs., 70
Scott, Jonathan, 15-17
Scoville bridge, 35
Scoville, Charles Burton, 35, 70
Scoville, James W., 34-35, 60
Scoville property, 59, 60
Scripps-Booth, James, 85
Seco Street bridge, 72
Secularization of missions, 14
Security First National Bank of Pasadena, 88
Serra, Junipero, 5
Shorb Company, 29
Shorb, James De Barth, 21, 23
Shoshonean Indians, 9
Showcase House of Interior Design, 66, 86
Silbey (early landowner), 31
Smith, Simon B., 28
South Pasadena, 16
South Pasadena Woman's Club, 85
Southern Pacific Railroad Co., 30
Southwest Museum, 88
Squatters (in Linda Vista), 22
Staats, William R., 63
Starr, Kevin, 84
Stock, Dr. Chester, 90
Stone, William J., 74

Teegarden, Jack, 57
Tefft, John Q., 71, 74
Test, Lawrence, 95

Throop Polytechnic Institute, 30, 82
Timkin, William Robert, 56, 72, 79
Tournament of Roses, 61, 63, 71, 92
Twilight Club of Pasadena, 88

United States census records (1890, 1900),
    46
Union National Bank of Pasadena, 90
"Upper and lower" Linda Vista, 31

Vail Mr. (and market), 71
Valley Hunt Club, 82
Van Every, C.B., 57
Van Pelt, Garrett, 65
Varner, Marion J., 75
Verdugo Boulevard, 19
Verdugo Canyon, 19
Verdugo, Catalina, 13-15, 17, 19
Verdugo City, 19
Verdugo, Jose Maria, 6, 10-13
Verdugo, Julio, 13-17,19
Verdugo, Maria Ignacio, 13
Verdugo, Maria Josefa, 13
Verdugo, Mariano de la Luz, 13
Verdugo, Teodoro, 14, 19
Vista del Arroyo Hotel, 63
Vroman, A.C., 89

Wachtel, Elmer, 83-84, 86
Wachtel, Marion, 83-84
Wadsworth, Hiram W., 64
Wakeley, Caroline, 70
Walker, Francis J., 62
Washington School (Pasadena), 68
Water concerns, 70-71
Watson, Mabel, 86
Watts, Charley, 22, 31, 36
Watts Tract, 23
Webster property, 58
Westridge School for Girls, 87
West Pasadena Railway, 32, 33, 40, 71
Whitcomb, G.F., 71

White, Margaret, 84
White, Nona L., 85
White, Orrin A., 84-85, 86
Wickham (early resident), 49
Wicks, Moses Langley, 21, 22; (real estate
    boom) 31, 36, 43
Wicks Syndicate, 22-23
Wildcat Canyon, 29
Williams (early resident), 49
Williams, James, 63
Williams, Paul, 92
Winchell, Annie, 71
Winston, Charlie, 36
Wood, Ella G., 67
Wood, J.W., 27
Woodbury brothers, 26
Woodbury Subdivision, 26
Woodruff, Charles, 49
Wright, E.T., 22

Yocum, Aaron D., 42, 43
Yocum, Arthur, 42, 43
Yocum, Hannah, 22, 23, 39; death, 43, 45
Yocum, Jane, 22, 42
Yocum, John DeWeese: (early years in
    Pasadena) 22-24, 26, 28, 29; as professor
    and citizen, 30; real estate boom, 32;
    Linda Vista bridge, 33, 34, 36; real estate
    "bust" and bankruptcy, 38-42; death, 43,
    44, 45, 46, 49, 50, 67, 70-71
Yocum, Louise, 42, 43
Yocum, Lydia Grissell, 22, 24, 41, 42
Yocum, Maurice, 42, 43
Yocum, Nathan P.: early years, 22-24; as
    businessman, 30; real estate "bust," 37;
    syndicate, 31; horse-drawn railway, 32,
    33-34; business problems and disappear-
    ance, 38-42
Yocum, Samuel, 22
Yucaipa Capital Corp., 74

Zimmerman, Frederick A., 86

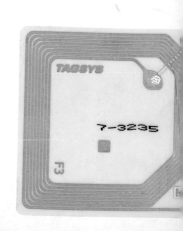